Quaker Adv

EXPERIENCES OF TWENTY-THREE ADVENTURERS
IN INTERNATIONAL UNDERSTANDING

Edited by
EDWARD THOMAS

Author of "Industry, Emotion and Unrest,"
"The Law of Chemical Patents," etc.

NEW YORK   CHICAGO

Fleming H. Revell Company

LONDON   AND   EDINBURGH

New York: 158 Fifth Avenue
Chicago: 851   Cass   Street
London: 21 Paternoster Square
Edinburgh: 99 George Street

PREFACE

THE stories told in this book were gathered, and edited for broadcasting, in the first part of the year 1928, at the request of the management of Radio Station WGL, of New York City. Almost all of the adventures were broadcast by the authors themselves.

The editor selected the speakers, took the place of some who could not appear, and revised the manuscripts. But each story sets forth the personal views of the author he selected.

His only regret is that some of the most interesting and thrilling adventures remain untold, some because the actors in them were too modest to be willing to tell them, others because the actors were not available in New York City.

EDWARD THOMAS.

New York City.

CONTENTS

I. THE BEGINNING OF QUAKER ADVENTURE AND
   ITS MEANING 9
      Edward Thomas

II. WITH LITTLE CHILDREN IN SILESIA . . . 23
      Harvey C. Perry

III. A DANZIG FOUR-LANGUAGE CONFERENCE . . 31
      Anna L. Curtis

IV. QUAKER RELIEF IN WARTIME FRANCE . . . 38
      Walter G. Bowerman

V. WITH THE WOUNDED AND THE PEASANTS . . 46
      Howard L. Carey

VI. AMONG REFUGEES IN THE WAR ZONE . . . 54
      Parvin M. Russell

VII. A QUIET NOOK IN TIME OF WAR 63
      E. Morris Burdsall

VIII. IN FRANCE FOR CHILDREN'S SAKE 70
      A. Gertrude Jacob

IX. ARMISTICE DAY AND AFTER 80
      James A. Norton

X. STILL IN FRANCE AFTER THE WAR . . . 89
      Alfred Lowry

XI. FEEDING A MILLION CHILDREN 96
      Frieda M. Burkle

7

XII. FIGHTING FAMINE 103
    Nancy J. Babb

XIII. ACROSS THE STEPPES OF RUSSIA 114
    Anna J. Haines

XIV. WHITE BANDITS IN RED RUSSIA 123
    Anonymous

XV. DOUKHOBOR PILGRIMS TO AMERICA . . . 131
    Howard W. Elkinton

XVI. JAPANESE BANZAIS FOR AMERICANS . . . 139
    Thomas Elsa Jones

XVII. IN THE PENNSYLVANIA COAL FIELDS . . . 146
    Sophia H. Dulles

XVIII. WITH FAMINE AND SCOURGE IN SYRIA . . . 156
    Eleanor W. Taber

XIX. RELIEF FOR SERBIA'S UNDERNOURISHED . . 165
    Samuel Ely Eliot

XX. AMONG AMERICAN INDIANS 175
    Lawrence E. Lindley

XXI. IN WAR-TORN IRELAND 183
    William W. Price

XXII. FOR GOOD WILL IN NICARAGUA 190
    Carolena M. Wood

XXIII. HAITI AND THE AMERICAN OCCUPATION . . 197
    Paul H. Douglas

XXIV. A WELCOME TO NANKING 204
    Edith M. Pye

XXV. ADVENTURES THAT HAVE NOT BEEN TOLD . . 211
    Edward Thomas

I

THE BEGINNING OF QUAKER ADVENTURE
AND ITS MEANING

THE clearest explanation of Quakers and their adventures came to me last summer in a train leaving Cuzco, the ancient Inca capital of South America. I saw in the seat across the aisle a lady from South Africa reading a guide-book, the best guide-book to South America. We had met her in the streets of Cuzco, looking at the long foundation walls of square-cornered Inca masonry, and at the carefully-carved, many-sided stones in the remains of pre-Inca masonry walls, so I ventured to ask her if she knew we were running along the Urubamba River, one of the head-waters of the Amazon.

She laid down her book, looked out of the window, and answered, " Why, no." Then I asked if she had noticed the threshing-floors, near the broad and rapidly-flowing river, where oxen were treading out the grain. She had not seen these, nor the winnowing parties of two or ten or twenty gorgeously-clad Indians throwing the trodden grain into the wind so the chaff was blown away, nor had she seen the reapers on the terraced mountain slopes, nor the gleaners. She had been too interested in reading her guide-book to see the world about her.

I never could have planned my South American trip without guide-books. I read the guide-books until I knew the route thoroughly, but I did not read the books when there were realities around me to see with my own eyes. A good guide-book follows the route the traveller is to take, telling him what he will see at each moment as he goes from place to place.

The great guide-book to the spiritual world, to spiritual realities, is the Bible. Countless people are so interested in reading the wonderful descriptions in the Bible that they fail to see the spiritual realities in the world in which they live. But many earnest souls have carefully studied their Bible and then, with it as their guide-book, have journeyed through the world seeing vividly the unused, almost unknown, spiritual powers in men. These souls have become leaders of men.

About two hundred and seventy-five years ago, George Fox took the Bible as his guide-book, and began to travel up and down England telling people about the light that lighteth every man that cometh into the world, adventuring out of his village. He was so enthusiastic in telling his story that he was thrown into prison. While he lay in prison, military leaders came to him offering him release if he would accept a captaincy in Cromwell's army, for he was a young man that year, 1651, during the Cromwellian wars. He refused the offer, saying, " I live by virtue of that light and power that takes away the occasion of all wars. I know whence wars come, even from the lusts."

His words make us think of the time when Jesus refused to use destructive force to overwhelm those who seemed to threaten the security of the kingdom of God, saying to the Apostle Peter, " Put up again thy sword into its sheath. Thinkest thou that I cannot now pray to my father and he shall presently give me more than twelve legions of angels? " And again, earlier in His ministry, He rebuked the disciples who asked that they might command fire to come down from heaven and consume those who did not receive Him, saying, " The Son of man is not come to destroy men's lives, but to save them."

George Fox, in taking the Bible for his guide-book, had no thought of creating a new church or sect. He was only seeking to take people back to the beginnings of Christianity. He did not even preach that war was wrong, but he preached the way of Jesus so effectively and so persuasively that many of his followers persuaded themselves that war was the wrong kind of adventure—that war was utterly wrong. They had seen too much of war, of the Cromwellian wars, to be content with attempts to theorize in defense of war. Both men and women among his followers sought other forms of adventure. They found a suffering and ignorant world around them, and they felt the burden of helping and teaching it laid upon them.

These men and women went up and down England preaching, and went into foreign countries, undaunted by any dangers. Mary Fisher's name is one of the best known, for after being flogged in Cambridge, England, and banished from Boston, Massachusetts, she, with some others, went to the Levant and succeeded in talking with the Sultan, finally coming home safe. They preached so powerfully that their hearers trembled, and the preachers often trembled themselves, so the new group came to be called Quakers.

Thomas Carlyle and others have jeered at George Fox and his followers for their uncouth spelling, but George Fox himself wrote the first English spelling-book, and it long remained the standard. Even in America, Benjamin Franklin printed an edition of it more than fifty years later, in Philadelphia. They founded schools, both industrial and academic. They established the modern sympathetic treatment of the insane, those unfortunate stricken people who hitherto had been chained or locked in dungeons. They found themselves leaders in prison reform and leaders in opposition to slavery and the slave trade.

And when wars came, as wars have often come, the Quakers sought to follow the path that Jesus took in His land which lay under the heavy heel of the brutal Roman soldiers in His day. As Jesus went about with healing in His hands, so have the Quakers sought to heal.

The story is long and covers many wars; in every war the first help for innocent sufferers came from quiet, earnest, thoughtful souls among the Quakers, the last people in the world you would take for adventurers. Another time I hope you will hear something about the English Quakers and their adventures, but just now I will have time only to tell you a few incidents, and those will be mostly about the Americans.

At the beginning of the entry of the United States into the World War, in 1917, a few Quaker young men felt called upon to refuse to bow to the government officials enforcing the draft law. A fund of five thousand dollars was raised to bring a hundred of them to a college near Philadelphia and train them for six weeks in the methods of relief work.

Within five years the enterprise had grown until the hundred had become almost a thousand men and women workers, and the five thousand dollars had grown to some twenty million dollars which was expended in relief. Beginning with work in France, the field expanded into Belgium, Italy and Serbia, and after the armistice spread over Germany, into Poland, Austria and Russia, to say nothing of smaller amounts of work elsewhere. Some of these trained workers were in Japan at the time of the great earthquake, in 1923, and had relief work well organized before nightfall on the day of the catastrophe, days before any other organized work was under way.

I wonder if you draw the same lesson from the Quaker work that I have drawn from it. If a single Quaker relief worker had gone to Europe and come back unharmed after working two or three years in hostile lands, it might have been called a remarkable phenomenon. But nearly a thousand unarmed workers went to Europe, and none met a violent death, nor did any lose any goods worth mentioning through robber bandits. The adventurous experiment of going unarmed was tried a thousand times and never failed. A scientist would call this a demonstration by the scientific method that security lies in adventurously going unarmed in the spirit of good will.

This scientific method required courage. On the last Sunday in May, 1922, a mid-west Quaker preacher serving in Russia during the great famine, saw a long line of horsemen coming over the steppe toward the house where he was standing, in a village, three hundred miles northwest of the Caspian Sea.

He soon saw the horsemen were Kurds, cousins of those who had massacred the Armenians for centuries. When they came near they said to the Quaker workers, " Where are your storehouses? "

The workers pointed to them.

" Let us see what you have in them."

The Quaker workers opened the doors, and the horsemen dismounted and looked at the bags of flour, beans, cocoa, and rice, and at the cases of tins of condensed milk, and saw that many of the packages were marked with the same red and black star that the Quaker workers wore on the left sleeve of their coats.

" You brought these goods from America to feed hungry people, didn't you? "

" Yes."

" You came all the way from America to feed hungry people, too? "

" Yes."

The horsemen looked at the food, then they turned to the Quaker workers, saying, " Well, you stay here and take good care of the people."

And they rode away.

Sometimes the adventurous unarmed workers can do more than merely protect food.

A boy of hardly twenty came from near the Dismal Swamp in Virginia to Pec, Serbia, and was assigned to drive ox-carts loaded with food over the rough, lonely mountain roads between the sea and Pec or Monastir. He was offered a military guard. He refused it, saying, " I didn't come here to have people shot for wanting what I have."

" But you will not be safe without it. Bandits will interfere and want to seize your goods," the authorities said.

" I refuse to tempt people to be shot."

" Your blood be on your own head! "

So he drove his ox-cart, piled high with provisions, back and forth unarmed. But one day bandits did interfere. On a lonely mountain road in the forest, mountaineers met him, saying, " Stop. We need what you have there."

The boy replied, " You don't want this, and it isn't mine to give. I am taking these supplies to starving people. I need help. Will you help me? " And they became his helpers.

In cities sometimes events took another course. At the time of the great " putsch " in Berlin, in 1921, the Quaker workers sat in their second-story office, in the house with their supplies, while the mob raged outside. The concierge knocked on the door. " There are a party of Communist soldiers down-stairs. They say they have come to guard your supplies. They say the government needs your supplies badly and will stop at nothing to get them. What shall I do? " The Quaker leader, an Englishwoman, said, " Bring them up here, if they want to come, but first they must leave all their arms in one of the empty storerooms down-stairs."

The Communist soldiers soon appeared, without their arms, at the door, fine-looking young men, with determined, hopeful faces. They seated themselves at the request of the Quakers, and animated conversation soon began.

Another knock came at the door. The concierge said, " There are a party of government soldiers down-stairs. They say they have come to guard your supplies. They say the Communists need them badly and will stop at nothing to get them. What shall I do? "

The Quaker leader said, " Bring them up here, if they want to come, but first they must leave all their arms in one of the empty storerooms down-stairs."

The government soldiers soon appeared, without their arms, at the door, massive, well-built men, in full uniform. They were introduced to all present, including the Communist soldiers, and all talked pleasantly together.

The foregoing are not extreme instances. They happened because every day people had the adventurous faith to trust to their idealism. The word Quaker means nothing under such circumstances, but the adventurous faith that enables men and women to dare to go unarmed, saves them and saves their opponents.

The Near East Relief announced a few years ago, when one of its workers had been killed, that in the first seven years of labours no worker had met a violent

death.   The management advised workers to go unarmed, but, unlike the Quakers, did not require it.
The Near East Relief workers tell of daily encounters
with bandits, but even in the wilds of Asia Minor, they
lost nothing by robber bandits, and the scores of workers spent $40,000,000 before that first worker met a
violent death, and perhaps he was armed.

When one of the foregoing stories was told at a New
York dinner table, a lady spoke up, saying, "Such
things don't happen in New York."

"Yes, they do," said her husband, a physician.   "I
was called over to the gas-house district about five
years ago, to see a sick woman.   Just off Tenth
Avenue, a man accosted me, saying, 'Stop, we need
your pocket-book.'   I looked at him and replied, 'You
don't want to keep me here.   I am going to see if I can
help a very sick woman up-stairs in that third house
over there.'   'No, we don't,' said the man, 'we will
see you safely out of here.   It is a dangerous place.
My partner here will watch at the door.'   They did
this, waited till I had done what I could for the woman,
and then escorted me to a respectable part of the town
and shook hands, saying, 'Good night.'"

There is difficulty in persuading the world that the
way to scientific security lies in going unarmed, because we have not learned to write the stories as they
should be written, as adventure stories, and because
editors fail to publish them, doubting if they will
interest people.

In the summer of 1925, in an inconspiuous place on
its twenty-third page, the New York *Times* printed

the story of the treasurer of a large Jewish hospital bazaar.

On his way home his taxicab was stopped, and he found a revolver thrust into his face while the face behind the revolver said, " Here, we need that money you have there." The treasurer had fifteen thousand dollars with him, but he said, " This isn't my money, it's money for a hospital to help care for sick people. You don't want that money." The face behind the revolver turned to a companion with an unspoken query. The companion said, " No, we don't. Here's something for you," and threw in a ten-dollar bill.

It is evident that unarmed adventurous people, bent on unselfish work, need fear nothing. In a footnote to history you can read how a party of unarmed Quakers rode out into King Philip's camp when King Philip's War was threatening. They endeavoured to avert the impending slaughter. King Philip told them that the white people were ruining his young men, selling them strong drink, and that the colonial courts would not take the word of an Indian, even the word of a good Indian, against the word of a bad white man. He said the white people and their government would not live up to their agreements. More things were said, and the comment of one of those Quakers has come down in a book, saying that the war could have been averted if the colony had been willing to be honest.

We need people today with the same adventurous courage that William Penn had, for that failure to avert King Philip's War did not discourage him when he came to America seven years later. In almost any history you can read how he made friends with the Indians and how that friendship lasted as long as the Quakers ruled in Pennsylvania, over seventy years, and kept the peace.

Pennsylvania was not the only colony to rely on Quakers for safety. In the official records of the colony of New Amsterdam you can read how the Quakers were persecuted when they first landed, in 1657, the men being set to wheel heavily-loaded wheelbarrows back and forth in the hot sun, and the women cast into prison. But before many years the colony sheltered itself behind the Quakers, planting a barrier of Quaker settlements along the rocky ridge of hills ten or fifteen miles east of the Hudson, all the way from the seashore to Albany. That ridge is called Quaker Ridge to this day. Above Albany the barrier of Quaker settlements turned west along the Mohawk Valley and extended nearly to the Great Lakes. Here the Quakers met the Indians with good will, and the colony lived in safety. Nations would do well to plant good will settlements, rather than forts, today along their frontiers.

There are many other kinds of Quaker adventures, as some of the workers found during the great Russian famine of a few years ago, already mentioned, the famine which followed that summer when less rain fell in the valley of the Volga than falls in the Sahara desert. In the early spring of the year when the bandits had looked at the storehouses, a group of Quaker men and women, a thousand miles southeast of Moscow, were facing the problem of procuring horses for the peasants around them in the valley of the Volga. Without horses the peasants could neither plough nor cultivate their crops, so without horses they faced another famine, and during the famine which they had undergone ninety-eight horses out of every hundred had either been eaten by the starving peasants or had died.

The group of Quakers had sent out, a month before, an unarmed messenger toward Turkestan, on what one of the workers called the golden road to Samarkand, with fifteen thousand dollars to buy horses from the nomad tribes of central Asia. But no word had come from him, save a telegram so garbled that it meant nothing, and now they had to decide whether it was wise to send a second messenger on the same errand with more money.

They saw in their group a newcomer, a young man full of courage, of tact, of kindly feeling, and with wide knowledge of horses, who seemed the man sent by God for such an errand, and him they asked to go as a second messenger out in the unknown. Next morning, at four o'clock, long before daylight, the young man rode off alone, save for an interpreter, and unarmed, with fifteen thousand dollars sewed into his clothes, going out on the golden road to Samarkand. He passed by the Caspian Sea and went out on to the half-desert alkali plains and steppes of Asia, keeping on eastward, ever eastward, until he came to the ships on the Sea of Aral, and then he turned south toward Samarkand and Afghanistan.

And the group in the valley of the Volga hoped and

prayed and watched and waited. A month went by. They had no news of their messengers. Their hope almost turned to despair, and they discussed whether they should send a third messenger, and whether they could find another who had the courage, the tact, the kindly feeling, and the knowledge of horses needed for such an errand. They looked around among their group.

Then one day some horses arrived, then tens of horses, then scores of horses, then hundreds of horses, then horses by the thousand. Then the group knew that both of their messengers had safely traversed the golden road to Samarkand and had accomplished their errand. And the story of how the horses were divided among the peasants would make another interesting tale if there were time to tell it.

Besides the threatenings by bandits the Quaker workers in Russia lived in constant peril from dangerous diseases. More than a quarter of the American workers in Russia were stricken with typhus, and though all of these recovered, it was estimated that in parts of Russia more than a quarter of the native population died of that disease.

To the Quaker workers the words of the Ninety-first Psalm came with a new vision of truth, " I will say of the Lord, he is my refuge and my fortress, my God; in him will I trust. Surely he shall deliver thee from the snare of the fowler, and from the noisome pestilence. . . . Thou shalt not be afraid of the terror by night; nor for the arrow that flieth by day: nor for the pestilence that walketh in darkness; nor for the destruction that wasteth at noonday. A thousand shall fall at thy side, and ten thousand at thy right hand; but it shall not come nigh thee. . . . Because thou hast made the Lord, which is my refuge, even the most High, thy habitation: there shall no evil befall thee, neither shall any plague come nigh thy dwelling."

Almost a thousand workers went unarmed into all manner of dangerous places, and dealt unarmed with all kinds of men. So dangerous did relief work in Russia seem to men who sat in comfortable offices in America that the American Relief Administration refused to allow any woman to go under them into Russia, yet during the famine years half of the Quaker workers in Russia were women, and they went everywhere, as safe as the men.

There are Quaker adventurers today in Nicaragua or on their way home. Others have been in Haiti, and still others are in Mexico, in China, Japan, India, Central Africa, and in many other regions, such as Palestine, Syria, Albania, and Salonika.

II

WITH LITTLE CHILDREN IN SILESIA

HARVEY C. PERRY, *a merchant and manufacturer of
Westerly, Rhode Island, was in charge of the Quaker child
feeding in Saxony and Silesia at the time of the plebiscite
held by the League of Nations in Silesia to determine what
part should be German and what part Polish. No one was
prepared for the result, which showed the cities almost
solidly German and the rural districts almost solidly Polish,
making it impossible to draw such a line as was provided
under the Treaty of Versailles. Mr. Perry's experiences,
which follow, tell part of the result.*

TWO days after I had sent two American Quaker
women relief workers into Upper Silesia, all
Europe knew that every telephone and telegraph wire
had been cut, and eight railroad bridges dynamited
there, and that the Polish insurrection had broken
out in the German territory. Great was my relief
to hear that the two Quaker women had seen what
was coming and had made their escape by automobile. But I did not know what was to become of
the twenty thousand children and babies which the
Quaker mission had been feeding every day in Upper
Silesia.

While the result of the plebiscite was being con-
sidered, to settle the nationality of the country,
Poland, arguing that possession would be nine points

of the law and would influence the award, decided
to take what could be taken and to hold what could
be held. Through all these excitements it was my
lot to be in charge of the child feeding in Saxony and
Silesia.

In order to reconstruct what we could of our organization for child feeding, on May 6, 1921, with my
interpreter, I left my headquarters in Dresden for
Upper Silesia, which we reached by a temporary
wooden bridge over the River Oder.

Travel was dangerous. We were stopped twenty-
four times by Polish guards between Oppeln and
Beuthen, a distance of about fifty miles. Often no
guards were in sight. They might be picking the
cherries for which that country is famous, but after
we had passed they would run out and fire at us. With
squeaking brakes and dragging wheels we stopped
quickly. Usually Polish boys in their teens were in
charge, and they knew little about guns and less about
reading and writing. The guns were often pointed
recklessly at us when not carried by a sling over the
shoulder. We had been warned that the guards were
quick on the trigger. But any piece of paper, if it
bore the Polish stamp, let us through.

The Poles controlled all the country districts close
up to the cities. No trains were running. Industries
had been closed and railroad service stopped. Communication by wire was very difficult, and there could
be no travel from city to city except by Polish pass,
something practically impossible for a German to get.
When we arrived at Katowitz the streets were crowded

from early morning until after dark. Between ten and eleven at night, shooting began and people sought shelter. Rifles, machine guns, heavy guns, tanks, and grenades were all brought into play. French patrols went through the streets shooting into any open windows. The uproar continued until after daybreak. When I went out in the morning, expecting to see the dead being raked up, all was as calm and peaceful as usual—in Upper Silesia.

German police were unarmed and might not even carry sticks. The cities were burdened with refugees, who were given a small daily allowance of money. Stories of torture were numerous, and I know some were true. Most of the terrorism had been in the country districts and about the coal mines. I saw no evidence of mines working. The air in the industrial area was as clear as in Dresden. Polish flags flew from the German-owned mines. Schools were closed, workmen were idle; in Katowitz alone, a city of 80,000, there were three thousand two hundred refugees, of whom six hundred were children. One hundred thousand marks, appropriated by the city for their relief, were stolen one day; the next no relief was paid. Each family was supposed to get seven marks daily. I couldn't buy a dinner for less than thirty-five. There was no fresh milk, no butter, no margarine, almost no sugar.

Refugees were in a pitiful condition, mentally and physically, sick, wounded, terrified and starving, aged and babies. Large numbers brought nothing with them. Families were separated, the men lost or sent into Poland. Nursing mothers could no longer feed their babies.

Major Spiller, an Englishman of the Interallied Commission, conveyed a food train to Gleiwitz one day. The Poles stopped the train, took him off, and for half an hour a crowd of two hundred debated in great excitement whether or not to shoot him.* When the future looked blackest, he asked for a glass of beer. His calm demeanor calmed his tormentors. Then he suggested they choose either to allow him to proceed with the food train for their children or to shoot him and put the children in the churchyard. Finally Mr. Korfanty was appealed to, and released the Major. The Englishman was eight hours moving the train fifty miles.

Quaker feeding stopped first in the smaller towns when the streets became unsafe for the children to come to the feeding stations. Later this was true also of the cities. Cities were often several days without light or water. Spasmodically hotels would close for lack of food.

When we started out from Katowitz in our Ford car we fortified ourselves with a Polish insurrection pass. This, added to the United States flag and the Quaker red and black star, gave us protection, though we declined having a Polish insurrection seal stamped on our country's flag.

At Beuthen we found the French had taken many tons of our food. By conference with them and the British this food was replaced. We bargained with the French to let us ship our American food from our own warehouse. Then we bargained with the Germans to risk their lives running a locomotive and a few cars to Gleiwitz, and obtained a German promise to return to the Poles the stolen locomotive and cars after they were unloaded. This we accomplished when not another train was moving in the whole area.

In the country districts there was fresh milk for sale at low prices, but not a drop was allowed to enter the city of Katowitz. Babies were dying for lack of it. At the hospital where only sick babies were cared for, the baby specialist in charge told us that another two weeks without milk would kill sixty or seventy per cent of these children. We went to the hospital ourselves and saw the babies. It seemed impossible that such emaciated forms could live at all. They were receiving condensed milk, but this their weakened stomachs could not retain.

The essential thing was to get fresh baby milk and to get the feeding centres in the cities functioning again. The Poles had never been willing to serve on our joint Polish-German committees. Now we persuaded them they must attend meetings, if only for the sake of appearances. But the key to the situation was held by Korfanty, who was reported to be leading the insurrection, although the Polish government was giving him no official recognition. It was common prophecy that if he were successful reward would come. Two years later he was premier of Poland.

So to Korfanty we went, at his headquarters in a schoolhouse. He had lived for some time in America and could understand my language. He was friendly, offered his hand and a cigarette as well. Mr. Korfanty granted that he was not fighting babies, signed the papers for us and promised immediate orders to let milk pass.

Yet even his order did not bring immediate relief, for the super-patriotic Polish boys, unmindful of the suffering children, spurned the order with the remark that this was their war. But by June first we had the feeding started again. Five hundred quarts of milk were brought each day to our kitchen. Our committee distributed it to hospitals. The doctors received, modified and distributed it again. The feeding of the older children at the centres was also started by June first.

Travelling between these centres was still exciting work. Sometimes our passes passed us, sometimes our American flag, sometimes our red and black Quaker star, but sometimes it seemed the whole combination of passes would not let us get by. Once, in entering Beuthen, we ran directly into street fighting; our scared Polish chauffeur promptly stalled the car, then had to crank it, and drove us to the street intersection where the fighting was. Until we could be investigated, some of the fighting men covered us with their revolvers and rifles, and their companions fired up the street toward the centre of the town. Why none of the return shots struck us we don't know.

As we travelled from place to place, we never knew what new lines or outposts would be set up, where to expect barbed wire entanglements, or stretched wires set to catch our necks, and what new wreckage must be passed. At one typical barricade the street was trenched clear across except at the trolley track; barbed wire obstructed the street and sidewalks, besides broken-down wagons and all sorts of junk. Sitting comfortably on the bench near by were the Polish guards, one in a Polish uniform, the other in that of a German policeman.

We were the only foreigners in the whole area without military protection. Newspaper correspondents had found it too hot early in the game, and had left. Many of the sentries eventually learned to know us, and almost all were good-natured when they saw our papers plastered with six Polish seals. They were enjoying the excitement and freedom. There was one I remember, not over twenty years old, with very dirty trousers, patched on both sides, one patch almost gone. Jammed down in his belt was his long revolver, on his head an old cap pinned to the Polish colours; a pack of cards protruded from the pocket of his shirt, which was open at the neck. His trousers were stuffed into shabby gaiters that tried to cover still more shabby shoes. But he seemed to know how to handle his grandfather's revolver. In any case, he let us pass when he became convinced that we were real Americans, in an American car, carrying American passports, and doing Quaker relief work.

When we came out of Upper Silesia every one was amazed at our safety and at the freedom with which we had been able to move about. Our success was due to the reputation of the Quaker relief organization, and to the fact that we stuck to our own business and asked for only necessary co-operation.

At the border we found thorough British preparations to meet the situation, tanks, big guns and reinforcements. The British moved in, and the Poles retired without resistance or bloodshed, and Upper Silesia waited quietly and safely for the final decision, while the children, both German and Polish, ate and relished their " Quaker-Speisung."

III

A DANZIG FOUR-LANGUAGE CONFERENCE

ANNA L. CURTIS *was sent to Germany, primarily as a speaker on Quakerism, because only a few of the countless requests for speakers on the Quaker message could be cared for by the Quaker workers busy with the child-feeding. She has been executive secretary of her own Quaker Meeting in New York City, executive secretary of the group of Meetings scattered over New York State, known as New York Yearly Meeting, and has served on many important Quaker committees. She is well qualified to explain the purpose and motives lying back of Quaker work.*

I SPENT two years in Europe working for the Quakers under the American Friends' Service Committee. Most of this time I was in Germany, and my adventures were many and various, although not so thrilling as were those of the Quakers who went to Poland and Russia. And as I did not go until 1923, I did not even see a revolution, although all of us there expected to see one. Every letter from home in the fall of that year asked us if we felt safe. Every foreign newspaper had its tales of bloody street fights between the police and the hungry mobs of the cities. That was the time when the German currency was taking its headlong plunge into worthlessness. It was the grim every-day joke that you needed a wheelbarrow to take your money to market; but that you could bring purchases away in one pocket.

Money was paper in those days, paper of steadily increasing denominations. For nearly a year, I never saw a coin in Germany. And during that time, the one essential industry—again a grim joke—was that of the Government printing presses, which printed thousand mark notes one day, fifty-thousand mark notes the next, and jumped to million-mark notes the following week. But however many ciphers appeared on the slips of paper, they were never worth any more in American money. I paid three hundred marks for a breakfast roll the first week that I was there. Three hundred marks would properly be about seventy-five dollars, but at this time, it was about three-quarters of a cent in our money. The next week the bank-note which bought my roll announced itself as three thousand marks in value. But it was still worth only about three-quarters of a cent. And so it went on.

It did not matter whether you had had an income of five hundred marks a year, or fifty thousand, or five hundred thousand; you were equally ruined, if you had retired from business and were living on your savings, small or large. Labourers were paid twice a week, and sometimes oftener, so that they could rush to the market and instantly change their bales of paper into shoes or groceries before the money lost any more of its value. And still the paper money fell in value. In November, 1923, a gold mark, if there had been such a thing, was worth a billion paper marks. That was the time when hungry crowds broke into food-shops to save themselves from starvation. That was the time when one heard the word revolution on every street corner. " Do you think there will be a revolution today? " would be the casual greeting.

We all wrote reassuring letters back home,—and wondered what would be happening by the time those letters reached the United States. We recalled the exciting adventures of the Quaker workers who really saw a German revolution, back in 1919. One of them accidentally got in the way of a skirmish in the streets of Berlin, and lay flat on her face for a time, while the bullets whistled over her.

But nothing of that kind happened while I was there. The money was stabilized at last; what a man earned one day was worth just as much the next; the United States began its second task of child-feeding, and the Quakers were again asked to direct the work. Germany began to creep back to recovery.

As I said in the beginning, I had no such thrilling adventures as did my comrades in the more eastern countries of Europe. There was plenty of excitement, however, and the Quaker work took me into all parts of the country. Sometimes I would visit a great city; and a few days later, would be travelling across the most rural countryside, riding in fourth-class cars, in close companionship with quaintly-dressed peasants and their baskets of cabbages and live geese.

I have been the guest of cities, entertained at the town expense, and taken about in the municipal automobile. And I have sojourned with labourers' families, and small shop-keepers on dingy back streets. I became acquainted with the Youth Movement, attended some of the conferences, visited some of its settlements, and took an occasional recreational hike with its groups. It was a great experience for me to learn that I could walk twenty-five miles in a day, and be able to start out again on the next day.

Then, in 1925, I toured Silesia for the German Peace Association, speaking at ten one-night stands upon the Quaker idea of peace. I was the fourth in a series of peace speakers who traversed that district that year. There was General von Schonaich, the German general whom the war converted to peace. Professor von Quidde, who has recently received half of the Nobel peace prize, for his devoted efforts toward international understanding; Prince Max of Saxony, an eccentric who lived mostly on raw food; and myself, representing the Quakers. Those who attended all four addresses must have found variety in our peace ideas.

But, after all, I think that my greatest adventure was at Danzig, when I assisted in what was probably the first German-Polish conference since the war. This, of course, was quite unofficial, so far as the two governments were concerned. The Quaker centres in Berlin and Warsaw had arranged for it, and had carefully " hand-picked " a half-dozen from each country who were known for their eagerness for peace, and their willingness to co-operate. But even these chosen delegates refused to visit each other's country, for fear of boycott, loss of business, or the like. Danzig was neutral ground, and there we met, in a hotel of that city. There were seven Germans, six Poles, and four Quakers, carefully keyed up to try to avoid all mention of the Polish Corridor, Poland's twenty-mile-wide pathway to the sea, which cuts East Prussia off entirely from contact with the rest of Germany.

At our first session, our first job was to reduce English, French, German, and Polish to a common language denominator. Nobody spoke Polish except the Poles themselves, of course. But they all spoke French or German, or both. Some of the Germans knew French and some English. None of us Quakers knew both French and German. So whatever a German said was translated at one end of the table into English, and at the other into Polish. If a Pole spoke in German, it was translated into English; if in French, into both English and German. It was harrowing, but the best we could do. And all the Polish and German conferees were so ceremonious and polite that human nature could endure it for only a limited period.

The Polish Corridor broke into the conference. A German exclaimed, " East Prussia is completely cut off from the motherland. Think of her fears and sufferings." And a Pole retorted, " Think of the partition of Poland, and what Poland has endured for over a century." Half a dozen began to speak at once. They were springing up all around the table, beginning to throw words at each other, when one of the two Quakers at the head of the table rose to his feet. Gilbert MacMaster belongs to a Quaker Meeting in New York. He is a middle-aged man, getting just a little grey, and calls himself " just a plain business man." Perhaps he is only a business man, but he is a good psychologist, as well. He glanced around the table, and smiled at us all—he was the only person there who knew everybody else. " It is half-past four o'clock," he said. " Perhaps this would be a good time to have our afternoon tea."

He did not say a word about the Corridor. He did not need to. But everybody agreed with him. All those people were accustomed to their afternoon tea or coffee, with crackers or cakes; and I presume they were getting hungry and cross for the lack of it. We adjourned immediately. And over the teacups, the small mixed groups of Germans, Poles, and Quakers, could, and did, discuss even the Polish Corridor with equanimity and understanding.

Twenty-four hours later the conference closed, Germans and Poles vying with each other in expressions of friendliness and confidence. And they were no mere words. I can not explain a miracle; but I know that those two groups of suspicious people had forgotten the boundary lines, and had recognized one another as friends and comrades working for the same cause. They had named a joint committee for further reconciliation work. They had planned for further conferences, and the Poles had invited a German to Warsaw to give an address there. They had planned to build up internationally minded groups to correspond with each other.

And thus came that triumphant conclusion. We had conquered the handicap of a four-language conference. We had depended on the spirit of friendliness, and it had not failed us, in this great adventure at Danzig.

All the plans for greater understanding have been faithfully followed, and have succeeded beyond expectation.

The second conference took place some months later, in Warsaw, and began and continued in the spirit with which the first one ended. Free visas on their passports were given to the German delegates; a large reception to the delegates was held on the first evening, and a great public meeting on the third, while on another night the Germans were guests of the city opera.

Several young Germans attended this conference. Later they were able partly to repay the hospitality of the Poles by receiving a number in a week's camp and conference of German and Polish young people together with a few Quakers up in East Prussia on the shore of the Baltic Sea. Speeches, discussions, folk-dances and singing, and much friendly talk as they hiked along the shore, or sat around a campfire at night, made the young people who came together that week feel truly acquainted with others from across the boundary line. They went back to their homes to assert everywhere that those Germans, or those Poles, were " real folks," and pretty " good fellows," after all. They are carrying forward the high adventure of friendliness.

IV

QUAKER RELIEF IN WARTIME FRANCE

WALTER G. BOWERMAN is an actuary for one of the very large life insurance companies, which means that he calculates what rates to charge for insurance, and tells how the funds of the company must be invested to meet future needs. During the war, and for a time following the war, he was the treasurer of the American Quaker Relief Work in France, handling about a million dollars a year. The work varied widely in scope, and in kind, and it called for much patience and foresight in adjusting the funds to the different emergencies. Moreover, it was the Quaker policy to sell goods, where possible, on time payments if necessary, rather than to give the goods away. Thus funds were constantly coming and going in field relief work, in reconstruction work, in hospitals, and in co-operative stores, the latter opened to meet the exigencies of restoring normal peasant life with as little outside dictatorship as possible.

Into Mr. Bowerman's central office in Paris there came many perplexing problems, reflecting many adventures.

THE mission of service which the Society of Friends, commonly called Quakers, maintained during the war and afterward is more than an apology for the ancient historical position of the Quakers. It may point to a better way of dealing with acute international relations. When the great fire of war broke out in Europe the first step of the Quakers was to issue a message to men and women of good will, which affirmed their belief that the method of force is no solution of any question. They called upon those whose conscience forbade them to take up arms to serve in other ways in the great crisis. By the American Quakers commissioners were sent to Europe to study the field of service and formulate plans for relief work.

These representatives decided to follow the methods of English Quakers. One of the tasks would be, therefore, to manufacture demountable houses to be transported to the devastated regions and there erected. This was of great importance so that the people could again find a place to live and till their own land. It would also relieve the overcrowded conditions of other places. This plan had been put in operation by the English Quakers, the first body of whom had gone forth in November, 1914, wearing as their insignia the famous black and red star which the Quaker relief workers had worn in the Franco-Prussian War. Other work under way was the providing of the people with clothing, food and medical care.

It was into this great endeavour of relief and reconstruction that the American Quakers were fortunately able to throw their resources and energies. To use a commercial phrase, a triangular merger was formed between them and the Red Cross and the English Quakers; the name of their organization in France was the Mission of the Society of Friends. The Red Cross was very valuable in securing permits to travel and in transporting supplies. It was the Red Cross official in charge of all American civilian

relief work in France who said, " There is no group
of people from whom we have learned so much, or
from whom we expect to learn so much, as the
Friends." He also described this undertaking as the
most tremendously fascinating and stimulating opportunity human beings were ever called on to meet.

The central office of the Friends' work in France
was, of course, in Paris. Each group of workers
elected its own chief and within limits was self-
governing, but many of the problems were sure to
filter in to Paris. The work was divided into departments, each with its head, who was member of
an executive committee. Each department reported
monthly to the committee, and at this time a budget
for the coming month of work was made up. The
executive committee also included representatives
elected by the members of the Mission, who were
thus able to influence the policy and plans of the
service which it was theirs to render. The organization of this body of relief workers was in this way
a unique and practical experiment in democracy. The
total number of workers altogether was about one
thousand, of whom one hundred were women.

The deterioration of health among the civilian population in the devastated areas of France was appalling,
and became more serious as year by year the tragedy
accumulated. It was natural and right that the
Quakers should provide for the medical and surgical
care of the civilians left in the wake of the great war
tornado. The maternity hospital at Chalons-on-the-
Marne was established in the awful days of chaos

immediately after the first battle of the Marne. The importance of the city as a railway centre exposed it to furious bombardments, both from long range guns and from the sky. Many a child came into the world here amid the din of explosives and was greeted with noises which drowned its cries of wonder. By January, 1919, about eleven hundred babies had been born in the " maternity," and scores of little orphans had been carefully tended in the adjoining baby house. The death rate among mothers and infants has been remarkably low, lower than that of any maternity hospital in New York City. The Quakers have now endowed this maternity hospital as a permanent living memorial to their labour among the people of France.

A most complete, separately operated, surgical hospital was set up by an American doctor in an old château at the Marne headquarters of the Quakers. Modern equipment, electric lights and an operating table were installed, and the capacity was continually increased until, at the time of the armistice, there were one hundred beds and seventy-five patients. The total number of operations performed there was about twelve hundred, and they covered a wide range of ills. The surgeon was frequently confronted with patients in whom disease had through neglect run its course far beyond the experience of a physician in America. Yet there were only seventeen surgical deaths among the first one thousand operations.

The central aim of the Quaker agricultural work was to put the devastated land back into cultivation, to rescue the neglected areas from their forests of weeds and to repair the havoc of shell-holes and barbed wire entanglements. A large number of the American Quaker workers were first-class farmers. The most important thing to produce was bread-stuffs, and the Quaker men tried therefore to get as much land into wheat as possible. They were well supplied with modern harrows, tractors and gang plows. There were no fences or hedges between the fields, and therefore the Quakers could with this equipment plow very large sections at a stretch.

There was much to teach the peasants about how to live and work together. Centuries ago the farm-houses had been grouped into villages for protection, and very closely crowded together side by side; the need for this has long since been past, but the natural conservatism of the peasantry has clung to the old tradition of what a village should be like. The farm villages are therefore overcrowded, ill planned and unsanitary. Since the value of land varies with its distance from the village, it was necessary that each peasant should own some near by and some farther off. His land is thus parcelled out in small lots and is unsuited for growing large crops; he knows little about scientific farming, and above all he does not understand how to co-operate with others.

The value of the work accomplished may be esti-mated from the fact that the military authorities re-ported at the close of 1917 that the district in Quaker hands was the only section of the war zone which had been properly threshed. The Quakers moved from village to village with their machinery, often sleeping in the same room with the entire peasant family. They were thus unable to have their windows open to the fresh air, for, as Mark Twain once humorously remarked, the reason the air is so pure in France is because the peasants always sleep with their windows shut.

Relief was obviously one of the most pressing needs. The poor people were of three classes—those living in cellars in destroyed villages, those who had fled to other villages less devastated, and those who had been caught behind the German lines by the first swift advance and were later returned through Switzerland because they were too old, too young or too ill to be of any use. These last were coming through at the rate of about two thousand a day. To all these it was necessary to distribute adequate clothing and simple furniture. Household equipment and food were supplied to them at reduced prices, the receipts reinvested, and thus the money was pyramided and made to go further.

Among the old people and women who could not go out to work an embroidery industry was started. It caught on tremendously; a British museum asked for specimens to use as samples of the new domestic art being started among the French. In 1918, Christmas was celebrated in the war zone for the first time in four years; for this purpose a ton of candy was sent over from America. A member of the Mission, who had learned in India such tricks as needle swallowing, entertained the children, but cautioned them to use clothespins instead of needles if they should try that trick for themselves.

The demountable houses were manufactured in two factories in the foothills of the Alps. The lumber was supplied by the French government, and came in by trains from the nearby forests. The houses were generally of three rooms, although, as they were built in sections, they could be made either larger or smaller as need dictated. They were made of planed, matched boards and were double, with an air space between the inner and outer boards. The floors, too, were matched with tongue and groove. They were well supplied with windows and doors and, when constructed, were stained a pretty brown to harmonize with the roof tiles.

The actual construction of villages with these houses took place in the devastated regions. To avoid delays in transit men were occasionally asked to volunteer to take the trip on top of the load of houses from the factory to the point of destination. There were always plenty of men keen for this freight expedition, which had neither Pullman nor dining-car facilities. But when a member of the Mission was on the load the railroad administration never shunted the car to a side-track.

The construction group lived on the very frontiers of civilian life in the midst of débris and desolation. Sometimes they repaired broken roofs and made half-destroyed homes habitable; sometimes they found no houses complete enough to make repairs. Their chief work was construction of the demountable houses which came by motor truck from the nearest railway centre.

As the months passed the workers became much deepened in life and character; in man after man the result had been a richer nature and a more dedicated spirit. They had found themselves in their service. And yet they almost never talked about this inner change. Like those people in the parable, they might have asked with perfect simplicity, " When saw we thee hungry and fed thee, or thirsty and gave thee drink, or when saw we thee naked and clothed thee, sick or in prison and visited thee? "

V

WITH THE WOUNDED AND THE PEASANTS

HOWARD L. CAREY, *a research specialist in business methods for a telephone company, was the first American to enter relief work in France after the beginning of the Great War. Three days after he graduated from a mid-west college he sailed for Europe.*

New problems arose after America entered the war. The United States War Department lost his papers, and refused for over six months to let him resume relief work in Europe. As a man standing over six feet, broad-shouldered and muscular, he sets forth the conflict of his ideals with governmental methods.

QUAKERS have believed that the best way for men to live together is to live in a spirit of friendliness and co-operation. Suppose you held this belief and suddenly you found that many of the most influential nations of the world were engaged in the active waging of a great war. Suppose, further, that you were a young man of the age most suitable for military service, what would you consider your duty? This question was an insistent and personal one, particularly to young men who had been brought up in the belief of the Quakers that it is possible for men to live in such a spirit as to do away with all occasion for strife and misunderstanding.

This question was answered by young Quakers in

England in 1914. Within a few weeks after the out-
break of the war, relief work had been organized by
them and was being carried on for the civilian population in the northern tip of France and in the edge
of Belgium. Milk was supplied for babies and children, a scourge of typhoid was broken up, a hospital
was established, and medical assistance was rendered
to the civilians who had been bereft of all medical
attention because the doctors had been called into
military service. This service was done quietly, but
so effectively that Quakers were allowed to continue,
and eventually other forms of work were undertaken.

By the spring of 1915 American Quakers were
co-operating by sending money to help in the work
which the English Quakers were doing. Arrangements
had also been made to send a party of four young men
from the United States to participate actively in whatever way their services could be utilized. It thus happened that this group, of which I was one, sailed from
New York on June 19, 1915, for England.

Arriving in London, we took courses in first aid
work, first in London and later in a camp just outside
the city. Our training included short courses in
nursing, first aid treatment, bandaging practice and
stretcher drill. There were also discussion groups and
lectures on a number of topics, with route marches
and physical drills to put us in good physical condition.

In the early part of August, 1915, negotiations were
completed between the British Red Cross Society and
the English Quakers whereby Quakers were to furnish
the staff for one of the ambulance trains operating

behind the British lines in northern France. On
August 14 the first group of forty-five men sailed
across the English Channel and landed at Boulogne,
France. Proceeding by train to Abbeville, some fifty
or sixty miles southeast of Boulogne, our experience
as ambulance train workers started the next morning.
The four Americans had been granted special permission by the British War Office to be members of
the unit.

The train, which had been given to the Red Cross
by the United Kingdom Flour Millers' Association,
was splendidly built, of English construction. It consisted of seventeen coaches. Four cars were fitted
with beds swung on iron brackets. Each of these had
a capacity of thirty-six patients, with space on the
floor to place eight additional stretchers in case of
emergency, and on more than one occasion it was
necessary to take on the limit. Five other coaches of
the English compartment type, each having a capacity
of sixty-four, provided space for patients who were
able to sit up. One coach was fitted as a dispensary,
with an emergency operating room. Other cars were
used for sleeping quarters, kitchen and mess room, and
other needs incidental to the life of the staff personnel.
We became thoroughly familiar with both the inside
and the outside of the train by virtue of a continual
process of cleaning in order to keep the cars sanitary
and neat in appearance.

Within a few days we found ourselves in active
work, starting early one morning to take four hundred
sick and wounded men from the clearing hospitals

back of the fighting lines to base hospitals at Boulogne on the coast. We proceeded to stations just back of the front line, taking on a fresh load of wounded about once a week. During one period of sharp fighting at the front we made seven trips within ten days. One of the towns where we frequently took on patients was near Ypres, or " Wipers," as the British Tommies used to call it.

Patients of every description were placed aboard the train. Some were slightly wounded or sick. Some were so swathed in bandages as to be almost completely hidden. Once a dozen Indian soldiers were placed in my car, and although I used the most expressive sign language that I could invent I failed to persuade them that English food was eatable. Another time three wounded German soldiers were among those placed on board. They caused comment, but I saw no animosity against them displayed by the other wounded men.

While in garage, that is on sidings waiting orders, recreation took the form of hikes through the country. A sports club was organized to arrange for soccer games with teams from other trains and hospital camps. On one occasion during a game with a rival team an unexpected order came for our train to move immediately. Our boys gave a fine exhibition of cross-country running in a wild scramble across fields to catch the train, and all climbed on board safely.

We were ordered one day to scrub with special diligence, in expectation of an inspection by King George, whose special train lay alongside ours. Our only reward was a delayed and cold dinner, for no King George arrived.

We moved about over the country and saw the work of preparation everywhere, something of the movement of troops and the forwarding of supplies and equipment. I could but be impressed forcibly by the extent of the organization necessary to carry on the complex details of army work. I became convinced that if men would but use the same amount of energy and organizing ability in a different manner the course of human affairs would be immeasurably improved. The world would gain through the constructive abilities of the splendid manhood sacrificed in the destructiveness of war.

After eight and a half months of service on the train one of my American companions and I paid a brief visit to the hospital operated by Quakers at Dunkerque, in northern France. We then returned to London, bade farewell to our friends there, and returned to the United States. This was nine or ten months before Congress passed the declaration of war placing this country in the conflict.

Between this time and the spring of 1918 I gave careful consideration to the question of what I should do. As a boy in a Quaker home I had been taught that all war is wrong. My experiences and observations during my work abroad convinced me that war is absolutely incompatible with Christ's teaching and a Christian way of living. I wanted, if possible, to do something constructive. But I could not accept military service as the fulfilment of my idea of duty.

When called in the draft and sent to training camp I presented a statement of my position and made application to be transferred to the work of relief and reconstruction which American Quakers had organized and were carrying on in France in conjunction with the American Red Cross and with Quakers in England. After six months delay, I was transferred to the American Friends Service Committee in Philadelphia. New Year's morning, 1919, for the second time I set foot on the shores of France, this time at Bordeaux, in company with eight or ten other Quaker workers. From Paris we were directed to Dole du Jura, a town near the Swiss border. In this town a wood-working shop had been set up in a partially completed school building, construction on which had been stopped by the war. Our men had roofed over the part required for our purposes. The French government shipped lumber to this town. Here the boards and other timbers were sawed to proper dimensions. They were then nailed into sections to form part of demountable houses. These sections were stored temporarily and later shipped to different villages in the devastated area. People in these villages in the fighting zone had been forced to flee and were living as refugees in various parts of France.

In Dole, where we worked, about eighteen of these houses had been set up, six of them just across the street from our workshop. They furnished temporary shelter for refugee neighbours. Once each day we were accustomed to clear the shop of its accumulation of shavings and timber trimmings. The women of the small colony were sure to be on hand with baskets, bags, aprons and anything else available, to gather up the bits of wood to carry home for fuel. There was laughter, chatter and often an approach to a quarrel as they vied with one another to obtain the most and the largest pieces. One family had stored in their extra stock of shavings beneath the floor of the house. Unaccountably it caught fire one day, and would have destroyed the house entirely except for the aid of the shop workers, who quickly came to the rescue. Only slight damage was done, but the excitement and chatter could not be so easily extinguished.

In the devastated areas, as around Verdun and a number of villages in the Argonne region, such inhabitants as could get back returned to their native villages in the summer of 1919, and found everything destroyed. In some cases they lived in dugouts or in the rudest sorts of shelter. Usually the mayor or head man of the village was among the first to return, and through him we made arrangements as to the location and number of houses required for immediate need. The houses had two or three rooms, and the construction was so simple that the work of building could be done by men with very little experience. In some of the villages, it was found that arrangements could be made with the officers in charge of prison camps for the use of German prisoners to assist in our work. The Germans were very able workers and seemed pleased to help in this way.

Another feature of our work, a matter of most vital concern, was the providing of chickens and goats.

Destitute refugees returning to their villages needed live stock to help them start life over again. Workers were sent to the south of France to purchase goats and rabbits. The animals were sent north by rail, and a worker had to accompany and care for them. The disorganized railroad system, coupled with the stubborn nature of goats, made these journeys an experience long to be remembered. The enjoyment came in retrospect. Each of the thirty to forty goats in a French box-car had to be watered, fed and milked, with whatever facilities one's resourcefulness could discover along the way.

The distribution of the animals afforded more interesting situations. The whole population of a village gathered when a truck load arrived. Each goat was examined and discussed before the small purchase price was paid. In paying for the goats the peasant preserved his self-respect, even though he bought them on small time payments, as was usually the case.

Thus the work went on. Many other Quaker workers among the thousand who went over could tell you other stories of their own experiences in relief work in France, Germany, Austria and other countries.

VI

AMONG REFUGEES IN THE WAR ZONE

PARVIN M. RUSSELL *was educated as an engineer, and now is a statistical research expert for a telephone company. He was trained for relief work in the first group of one hundred brought together just after America entered the war. Thus he came to be in the war zone both after the advance of the Allies in 1917 and during the last German drive of 1918. Thus, also, he served in the Somme and the Argonne during the war, and helped in reconstruction in the Verdun area after the war. He can tell of only a small part of his work, which often lay between the French artillery and the German trenches.*

AN advance by the Allies in the spring of 1917 recaptured portions of the Somme in northern France. The Allied troops passed on toward the north. The whole countryside was a mass of tangled ruins, yet love for the shapeless remnants of homes soon brought the peasants back to live in cellars, dugouts, stables, or temporary shelters made of a few boards. It was into this region that a group of young Quakers came in the fall of 1917, to lend a hand in getting the people settled again. Some of the boys went off to southern France, bringing back car-loads of chickens, rabbits, and goats to sell in small lots at cost to the returning farmers. In some cases a house had been struck by shells but not wholly destroyed;

perhaps we could patch the roof and make a door, so that a family could be comfortable in it. Or, if the old houses were flattened out ruins, we could put up little portable houses of two or three rooms, that were made in southern France and shipped to us in sections.

Before the sunny fall days, many of the families were back, gardens were being cultivated, and there were several cows in our village. There was one young woman who used to gather sugar-beets growing wild out in the fields, and after loading them into a wheel-barrow, she would square her broad shoulders and wheel them to a farm a quarter of a mile away, where the beets were used as feed for a cow. In return she received milk and butter, and possibly a little money. There were few horses left for the farmers. Most of the cultivating of the gardens had to be done by hand. I have seen bent old women spading the dark earth for hours.

After the peasants of our village were all sheltered, we rebuilt one room of the schoolhouse, a teacher came, and the children learned to read, and write and, most wonderful of all, to sing again. The children were cheerful companions as they would come clattering down the road in their wooden sabots or shoes. The boys all wore black smocks over their regular clothes while at school and at play, so it was hard to tell which were boys and which were girls. They would often stand around and watch us, the strangers, work after their school was out, and at times they would make a game of carrying boards or tiles, or bringing tools for us. Many a little house was put up in quicker time just because these bright-eyed lads and girls added their energetic hands to the job. At Christmas time we gave them a party, with a sweater or doll or woolen gloves for each eager youngster; and the next day two or three groups of them appeared, with trembling dignity, to read us their notes of thanks.

Later in the winter the roads were blocked by a heavy snow. The baker could not get in to our village with bread, so we built a snow-plow from heavy planks and lengths of angle-iron. When the mayor's two horses were hitched to it, we opened the roadway to the outside world, while the children followed, shouting with delight over the first snow-plow they had ever seen.

All during these days the low rumbling of the distant cannons came to us. At night we dared not allow the tiniest beam of light to show from our windows, for the keen eye of an observer in a bombing plane needed only one gleam to help him locate his target. Then, one day in the spring, the booming of the guns rolled nearer, and at night the sky was pierced with rockets—Veery lights, the soldiers called them—like tireless fireflies.

Our village shook to its foundations as an aeroplane visitor, with racing motor, high in the air dropped five bombs near the French aeroplane sheds down the road. Morning came with the big guns still pounding away; the air was now pulsing with the roar of Allied aeroplanes; tired and disheartened troops filled the roads;

and a few hours later, as we were working on the roof of a barn, we looked across the fields and saw a plane, with a black cross under each wing, suddenly leave a trail of dark smoke, then dive toward the earth in flames as it paid its price for being too bold.

By night we knew that this village, where we had worked for five long months, could not be saved. Before dawn word came to our neighbours to pack up immediately and get to Montdidier, where there were trains for the southward. That twelve-mile walk to Montdidier threw us into an endless procession of families trying to escape with as many of their possessions as possible. Every kind of vehicle was used, from high two-wheeled farm carts to baby carriages— all overflowing with furniture, bedding, kitchen-ware, and children. Some people were trying to drive their cows along; others had scarcely enough energy left to keep going themselves; many of them had walked all night. Old men and women trudged along with bowed heads and painful steps; hungry, thirsty, neglected infants wailed; and in the eyes of these refugees was suffering and despair. When they reached the railroad station most of their baggage had to be abandoned, for there was no room for furniture or mattresses in the overcrowded trains.

After reaching Paris, for five weeks I spent my nights in the Gare du Nord or the Gare d'Ivry—two railroad stations in Paris—through which 40,000 refugees passed on their way from the war zone. Trainload after trainload of them wearily poured into the stations; they arrived, and they were directed into temporary waiting-rooms, where we served them heaping trays of bread, cheese, and sausage, with gallons of steaming cocoa. Sometimes they were given only a short rest; at other times they could wait most of the night, before being sent on to the south. Families would gather together and try to snatch a bit of sleep, propped against one another, or stretched out on the floor. Strange as it may seem, some of these peasants had managed to smuggle a dog, a cat, or even a goat into the crowded compartments of the trains and were taking these pets with them.

Few of these thousands of uprooted families knew where they were going. Unless there were special friends or relatives to whom they could go, they were forced to—just go on, being sent to southern France somewhere, and distributed among strange villages, where in turn the local mayors would allot them, trying to keep refugee families together; but in this cruel transplanting, few of the refugees found happy homes.

A few months later, in the summer of 1918, we were busy helping to erect a large one-room wooden barrack, as an annex to a Quaker surgical hospital for civilians at Sermaize. Patients were being placed in one end of the barrack before the other end was even covered. In the midst of this work there came a call from the French authorities to send every available automobile with two drivers to evacuate the section along the Marne River, east of Château Thierry, where hundreds of civilians in scattered villages were endangered by a new advance from the north. These villages were being shelled because the wooded hills around them on the south bank of the Marne were shielding lines of French artillery. The people were slow to leave, and it required the authority and even the presence of a French officer to make them realize that they must move out before they were killed.

For two weeks we made repeated trips into the villages, which lay in front of batteries of camouflaged guns, whose shells were continually whistling overhead. Here we gathered van-loads of peasants, taking them, with just a few of their bundles, out to a concentration point where the Quaker women workers gave them bread and soup and sent them on their way to safety.

At one small village we found that every one had fled, leaving a helpless woman fully dressed lying in a rotting bed with a serious infection. She had had practically no food for five days and absolutely no care. Two hardened French stretcher-bearers who had volunteered to help us move her gave up the attempt after seeing her repulsive and seemingly hopeless condition. One of them even said it would be a kindness to put her out of her suffering. We finally lifted her—bed and all—into our van, and delivered her to a hospital thirty miles away, where with good care she recovered. Throughout the whole journey we heard no slightest complaint from her.

Another day as we were guided by a French captain to an isolated farm we passed the remains of four horses, killed by a shell. At the farm the old people asked us to join in a tiny glass of some rare old cordial as a last farewell to their flower-framed cottage. So in the immaculate kitchen we stood together, silent because words had no place at such a moment, until each one with lifted glass murmured, " *A votre santè.*" We sipped the wine solemnly, for the deep suffering on the face of the old peasant woman had turned an ordinary ceremony of hospitality into a sacrament.

It was hard enough to smile in those days, but another woman, in spite of losing her home, turned to me with the light of excitement in her eyes, and said, " This is my first automobile ride."

The thought of these adventurous days along the Marne takes me back to a village that lay under the very eyes of a line of hostile sausage-balloons tethered just across the valley—twenty miles east of Château Thierry. Shells were falling at frequent intervals, and we had gone in beneath the muzzles of the French 75's with orders to bring out all the remaining civilians. After winding through lines of dusty troops we stopped in the shelter of a building which hid us from view.

We had soon collected nearly every one from the houses nearby when an elderly man came running up, threw his sack into the auto-van and commenced to climb in with the others. When safely inside, he confided to me that his wife was still back there, but that she refused to come away. He had explained the urgency of the situation to her, but without effect, and as far as he was concerned, why should he risk his life any longer just because she was such a stubborn, unreasonable old—well, he was going to abandon her, and that was settled!

By this time I was eager to see his obstinate wife; I thought she might be persuaded to come, after all. So Monsieur led me down the road to his home, pointed to the kitchen door, and stood aside to see what happened. As I opened the door, Madame was sitting stiffly in a straight chair, looking at the blank wall, nor did she change her position one hair's breadth as I urged her, because of the shells that were falling all around her home, and the lack of food, to join her husband while our car was there. But she was immovable; true, death might come hissing through the air—she was not afraid. The food made no difference; if she lived she would find some, somewhere. Monsieur could go if he desired, but she would not move a step.

Her whole spirit had risen in rebellion against this insatiable, heartless Force that had already taken much that she held dear, and now was tearing her away from the homely village where all the roots of her being clung tenaciously, determinedly. Her revolt was far more than desperation. There was a calm nobility in her quiet eyes, and every line of her sun-tanned face was set heroically.

Monsieur returned with me to the waiting automobile, expecting to make his way to safety as soon as possible. He was half angry when I told him that he had no right to leave his wife after their many years together: that the only fair thing for him to do was to go back and stay with her. He was willing to wait after I promised to come back for them the next day.

The fact that they did come out the following morning can never dim the remembrance of that grey-haired peasant woman's courage. It was as if she, like Joan of Arc, had heard still voices speaking and, in that hour of fearless rebellion, had lived the prophecy of an enlightened world.

VII

A QUIET NOOK IN TIME OF WAR

E. MORRIS BURDSALL *is another of the tall, stalwartly built, Quaker young men who fearlessly faced the clash between his ideals and governmental methods. He, too, was trained for relief work in the first group of one hundred brought together just after America entered the war. Though he happened to be assigned to a quiet part of France, his experiences convinced him of the need for people who would serve the world in its great need, and since the war he has studied medicine.*

IT seemed like being transported to an earlier age to live with the Quaker boys in the little French town of Ornans, in the foothills of the Jura Mountains, a short distance from the Swiss frontier, during the winter of 1917-1918. We had already taken a few steps back in time, crossing Bordeaux a-la-horsecar directly upon our landing, and riding overnight in railroad cars which could claim nothing in common with a Pullman, unless possibly their wheels. The wartime Paris where we stopped en route had long since given over its efforts to keep up-to-date to the more urgent one of holding the Hindenberg line. It moved about on foot, in hacks, or pre-war street-cars. Eyes were pinned only upon *communiques* which bore news from the front. But at Ornans, barring a few twentieth century importations, we had slipped back a hundred years. Outwardly, too, the world was at peace, if one did not notice that the population consisted only of women, children and old men, with an occasional blue-uniformed poilu.

A peasant town, Ornans, was one of thousands of its kind in France. Old houses, bunched together, hemmed in a few narrow streets, with sidewalks, if any, scarcely wide enough for one healthy American foot to pass another. The street pavement was usually mud, on a foundation of cobblestones. The department of water supply consisted of a few scattered fountains ever flowing with mountain water, surrounded by stone scrubbing-basins for laundry work. The swift Loue River flowed through the town, and many of the houses hung over its banks. Every few days the town crier walked through the streets, using a big drum to gain attention. It was all the inhabitants could do to understand him, and a hopeless task for us. Domestic animals shared the dignity of the town, being driven in each night from the surrounding farms on which there were no buildings.

The rugged country inspired the art of Courbet, one of France's great painters, born at Ornans. The valley had a depth of four hundred feet. The hills, topped with cliffs on either side, were terraced and planted with crops. Down stream a few miles the ruins of a château, dating back to 900 A. D., stood out on a bluff. Ten miles up stream, the valley narrowed and deepened into a canyon where the river flowed from a cave in the mountains. This canyon was, with us, the objective of a favourite bicycle trip on Sundays.

Our shops for manufacturing two- or three-roomed, portable houses for refugees—or *demontables*, as the French call them—were located on each side of the stream in Ornans. The window-frame and door mill was run by two great water-wheels and manned by our most experienced carpenters. Another wood-working shop, equipped with American machines, and the assembly room for making the house sections, were well organized for rapid production.

Here from twenty-five to fifty English and American Quaker boys, with the red and black Quaker star on their left arms, lived and worked together for a year. Our home was an old pre-war absinthe distillery, a three-story concrete building. The first and second stories were heated by stoves and used as general living quarters, while on the third we made good use of our army cots and sleeping-bags. Breakfast was prepared by two of the group chosen as orderlies each week by the head of the group. Other meals were cooked by a French *Madame*. The orderlies often had to break the ice in the great hogsheads to secure water for the morning ablutions. The favourite indoor sport such mornings at breakfast time was to secure space around the stove to toast our war bread and, incidentally, to toast ourselves.

We had many unforgetable experiences. After the day's work, in spring and summer, the children gathered for games and stories in front of our house. We found their French easier to understand than that of the older folks. We found, too, that their childish interest, and mischievous pranks were those of our

American children or of children the world over. Some
three hundred of them sat wide-eyed at our Christmas
party in the town's largest hall. After our show we
passed out paper bags, containing an orange and some
sweets, to the children as they left, but a few of the
boys were good at hiding their bags, dodging in by
another door and coming out a second or third time.
The dear old *Curé*, or priest, who is invariably every
one's godfather in such a community as Ornans, must
still bear the marks of his efforts to maintain law and
order among his charges that evening.

In the evenings we became acquainted with many of
the village families by exchanging English lessons for
French. Some of our group had considerable difficulty
with the language. One of them once tried to ask a
woman the age of an old church, but instead asked
what her own age was. When she replied, " Sixty," he
immediately said, " Oh, no, six hundred! "

The war was often brought close home to us by
tragedies in these families. The brave little *Madame*
who operated the public baths and kept them open
during the winter months for our special benefit, had
been supporting her three little tots since the time when
she had lost all word of her husband, four years pre-
viously. Speaking of baths, the children's clothes were
often sewed on for permanent use during winter. We
had good authority for the report that a certain man
of seventy-five years had recently died from the effects
of a cold. He had fallen in the river one autumn day
and could not resist the irritations from his first bath.

Those of us who had worked steadily for nine

months or more had ten-day furloughs. These were usually spent in sightseeing. In September, 1918, six of us went to Chamonix and climbed Mount Blanc, 15,780 feet high, the highest of the Alps. The summit is in France, but parts of the slopes are in Switzerland and Italy. At eight o'clock on the appointed morning we started on our two-day trip and reached the edge of the first glacier at lunch time. Here we put on dark glasses and stepped out for the first time into a region of eternal snow. Crossing this glacier was easy going, and we soon came to the juncture of the two great glaciers. We were roped together here in three caravans, each including a guide. At this place the ice shifts so often that a path a week old is obliterated, and our guides showed great skill by making our way across and up to the Grand Mullets, the half-way shelter, without once retracing their steps. Although many crevasses were apparently bottomless, all were sufficiently narrow to step across at the proper place. At four o'clock P. M. we reached the Grand Mullets, a ten-room house on the side of a pinnacle of rock at 10,000 feet, surrounded completely by snow and ice. After a good hot meal, prepared by the guides, we watched the sunset and then turned in for sleep.

We were wakened shortly after midnight and were off again on our climb by two o'clock, to be down off the snow again before it should get soft in the afternoon, when avalanches might occur. The wind felt icy at first, but soon the exercise warmed us, and we trudged upward trusting implicitly in our guides, whose lanterns had been blown out a few minutes after starting.

The silence was oppressive, broken occasionally by a sudden crack from distant ice cliffs followed by the rumble of sliding snow. At times we could still see behind and below the friendly lights of Chamonix.

After what seemed years, dawn appeared, and soon the pink of sunrise lit the summit. Gradually the growing colour travelled down the snowy slopes to meet us. We were warned to keep silent in crossing one of the flat plateaus, as the vibration of our voices might loosen the overhanging snow on our right. Upon reaching the ridge at the foot of the great dromedary's hump, we rested an hour and had lunch. From here on, the guides cut steps almost continuously. At the steepest parts we easily touched the snow ahead while standing erect. On either side the surface sloped off twenty or thirty feet, then disappeared, to appear again some thousands of feet below. Shortly before eleven o'clock we reached the summit, a flat space about fifteen by one hundred feet. The descent was more rapid.

During the summer of 1918, I assisted in erecting thirty of our demountable houses at Besanscon. This little *cité* was put up to relieve congested living conditions among the refugees who had been driven from the war zone. People in America can scarcely understand refugee life. We found, for example, a widow with several children living in two rooms, while a son of the sister, who had gone insane at the front, was most of the time in a state of complete paralysis on a bed in one of the rooms. This refugee family was placed in one of our houses. I had the good fortune last summer to visit this group of our houses; I found them still useful, some being utilized as a home for tubercular children.

The spirit of this war-time service was in part expressed in the following verses by Griswold Williams, who worked in the window-frame mill at Ornans:

" *I've not made doors and windows for châteaux or*
    palaces—
Only for little wooden demountables
To shelter mostly simple folk
Dripped from the grinding jaws of War.
Red tiles will be for roof, the walls be brown, and
    green the white-knobbed doors.
The sections bolt together easily,
As barren as a shed for animals almost,
Until my doors and windows make it—home. . . .

" *O patient Master Workman of the world,*
Shaper of all this home of human kind!
Teach me the truer trade of making doors and windows
    for men's souls:
Windows for letting in love's widening dawn,
Doors swinging outward freely on Truth's pleasant
    ways."

VIII

IN FRANCE FOR CHILDREN'S SAKE

A. GERTRUDE JACOB, *for many years a teacher of physical training in the public schools of New York, obtained leave of absence when America entered the war, and went to France to throw her knowledge of hygiene into the problem of caring for the children, the innocent sufferers from war. She speaks from a broad experience with children. She has travelled the wide world over, has seen children in South Africa, in Japan, in China, and many other lands. In France she first went to the Quaker hospital in the Marne, close to the battle line.*

FRIENDS of the unseen audience, I call you friends for, when human souls touch one another in a common compelling interest, a tap root of friendship is established. The adventure of which I am going to speak is about our little war victims, many of them but tiny waifs of humanity, whom a cruel world had robbed of the rights of childhood. Deprived of food for their growing bodies; deprived of fathers and perhaps of mothers; living in basements under the débris of what once were smiling homes; shivering with cold in winter; enervated by the moist heat of summer; suffering pitifully from nervous systems wrecked by the constant noise of bombardments, they will make an appeal to all who love children. Where are those babies now?

One lies under the poppies in northern France. Death was kind when it gave her an early grave. She had been ill for a year before she came to our Quaker hospital in the Marne. She was so tiny that at once we christened her Midget. Her mother said that they had been driven from their home and that, after wandering around four days, they found a well and drank from it. The water proved to be contaminated, and Midget had been poisoned by it. She was now four and a half years of age and weighed but thirteen and a half pounds. She looked so frail that we were almost afraid to put her in a bathtub, for fear she would break when lifted up. At first she could not stand alone, and her face was wizened and old.

But her eyes! I was captivated with them at first sight. Those two beautiful, sleepless, brown eyes seemed to see things far, far away, as they stared out into the strange hospital ward and at the queer-looking beings dressed in grey uniforms, with big white aprons and kerchiefs folded over their heads, who were forever walking around and seemed to be watching her. Stranger yet, one of those queer-looking beings offered her something to eat soon after she arrived. It was a sloppy mixture of bread and milk such as *maman* had never given. Then independence asserted itself, and the queer beings were shown that even in a small emaciated body will power still lived. Why should she eat food when she did not like its looks? One sweep of the hand, and over onto the floor went the distasteful mixture! Did it matter to her small soul that a brand-new, flowered comfortable was not improved by sticky mixtures?

At first Midget had to be placed in a regular hospital bed, in which she looked lost, she was so small. She would have had ample room had she slept upon the pillow only. One happy day a cot in my children's ward was vacated, and then began the guardianship which deepened into an intense love for the afflicted child. Her case at first seemed hopeless, but through the interest of the kind man in Paris who sent supplies to us we were able to get some life-giving fruit for her. The children's craving for fruit was so intense that when I pared apples for Midget, the other little ones would stand around and beg for mouthfuls of the skins. They never fought with each other for this dainty; they just stood patiently waiting with hungry eyes to see if there would be enough to go around for a second time.

Slowly Midget began to gain until she was able to walk, and even play in the sandpile with the other children. She objected very much to her special diet. For meals, our little ones would sit on the floor at the low bench which served as a table. One day Midget was with me on the other side of the room when the bench was brought in. Suddenly I gasped. The child who was so uncertain of her footsteps that she usually had to be led, shot across the room and seated herself with the other children. Then she turned around and looked at me—as much as to say, " *Now* you cannot stop me from eating what I want! "

Midget's patience and sweetness had a persuasive

effect upon us all. Children vied with each other in helping her when she walked; adults, in passing, would try to win one of her beautiful smiles; and maids from all sections of the hospital were always ready to talk to Midget. Who shall say that she lived in vain even though she was but one of the thousands of tiny war victims!

One of the chief delights of the children in our Marne hospital was to drive with the man for the daily supply of milk when a nurse had time to go with them. Our Marie suffered so from her eyes that she often had to wear bandages and be kept in a dark room. She was a reticent wee thing, made the more so by her semi-blindness. One day when I was taking Midget for the envied drive I tried the experiment of taking Marie, too. The effect was magical. The child from whom we could scarcely drag a word indoors talked to the horse with the greatest abandon. For a while nothing else existed for her. " *Allez, Coquette,*" " Go quick, Coquette," rang out over and over.

Then Marie burst into song, learned in part from the phonograph records which we had bought with money supplied by kind American friends when they learned that little children had to be taught to laugh amidst the gloom of war surroundings. Clear and loud her baby voice rang out. She could not see the surprise and the answering smiles she awakened from passersby, but for once her child soul was as free as the birds of the air. She, too, did her bit, and I do not doubt that today she is in the land where children do not have to suffer.

Another day I took a group of children walking. By way of recreation they sang prayers for the dead— poor little souls! They had had no music except what they heard in churches, and the greater part of church music was given over to prayers for the dead. The best young men had gone from every village and hamlet in France, and there was scarcely a family which was not in mourning for some relative or friend.

As an antidote for the appalling gloom I started a recreation class for our adults in the hospital. Before a week had passed we were listening to the noise of bombardment from the Château Thierry drive. Our helpers had no heart for anything. They were reading what meagre news they could get and anxiously scanning the lists of the dead. Women as well as children bear the brunt of war. The best supplies, the best medical men, and the best nurses must go to the maintenance of the army. The suffering behind the lines, the struggle for existence, the constant burden of worry and anxiety belong to the weaker sex. Of the courage of soldiers we often hear, but it was no stronger than the courage of the mothers in war-torn France. Theirs was the daily, hourly round of anxiety, not only for their boys at the front, but for the keeping together of the family at home. From early in the morning until late at night they toiled in the fields, using even pick-axes in breaking up the baked shell-torn soil in what once had been fertile farm land. They could not know what would happen to their children while they were away. Such is woman's contribution in time of war.

Now visualize, if you will, the south of France and the beautiful scenery of the French Alps, where we had a pre-tubercular hospital in the little village of Samoens. The afternoon of which I wish to speak was particularly dank and dismal. The rain had been pouring in torrents, until the children, worn out with being housed up all day, grew quarrelsome. Life in France at best is very different from life in America, where children have so many toys. Our French youngsters did not have even a play-room. The dining-room was used for that purpose when not needed otherwise. With a family of over ninety, however, it was principally " otherwise."

It takes time to eat when, because of the crying need of mineral-starved bodies, eating becomes almost an obsession. It takes time to set tables and clear away dishes, and to sweep up floors. There were few hours, therefore, that could be devoted to play even if the dining-room had been conducive to the play spirit. There was a lack of ventilation. Even on bright days but few rays of sunshine found their way into the old building which we had to utilize. There were ugly walls, odours of ancient days. Tables and chairs were always in the way against playing good romping games. Only one end of the room was ever warm. The small stove but served to emphasize the dreariness, for it was black inside, and the fire was out a good part of the time. It is difficult, you know, to keep a fire going on coal dust.

On this particular afternoon I was feeling as disconsolate as the weather. Home seemed so far away and the outlook so hopeless. There were the men out in the trenches dealing death and destruction. Here were we with their wives and children, brought back from prison camps across the border or rescued from squalid surroundings after having lost all through the tide of war. It suddenly occurred to me that I might do something to cheer up the children. I descended to the bleakness of the dining-room and invited the youngest to come to the warmth and the slight touch of home which my room possessed.

I felt guilty in having the luxury of a miniature stove in my room, but it was a necessity. I was so ill from the sudden plunge from our furnace-heated houses to the rigours of winter in the French Alps that our doctor refused to allow me to occupy a room, as I did at first, devoid of either sunshine or heat. It had been a new experience to me. I had had to keep my hot-water bottle near at hand while dressing because I could not comb my hair without thawing out numbed fingers, and I had to empty the bottle, when through, because of the danger of its freezing and bursting. However, I shared my heated room with any member of the staff who wanted a warm place to sit, so that it really served as a club room. To the babies I am sure that it represented something akin to Paradise.

Eagerly they came, klipity-klap with their wooden shoes, up the stairs and beheld with bated breath the glories which awaited them. A table was improvised from a suitcase, and a piece of white paper was used for a table-cloth. That in itself was a luxury, for white wrapping paper was almost unknown in France at the time. I had been sent a small box of crackers in a package from home, and I had been able to buy some apples in the village. I could not allow each child more than one cracker and one piece of apple in order to have the meagre allowance suffice for the older children, too. When we had finished I made paper caps out of the table-cloth, and it was a very cheerful group that finally clattered off for their evening meal decked in the newest style of head-dress and eager to show themselves to their less fortunate comrades.

I had an evening class in recreation, and I had planned a party for them, too. After the babies had gone to bed, I found when I reached the dining-room that something was wrong. Poor little René, who always had to wear a Capuchin hood because his nerves had been so wrecked by the noise of the many bombardments he had been in that he could not bear even ordinary sounds, was being branded as a thief. He had every evidence of guilt, for he was trying to hide something in his pocket, and fright was depicted in every line of his pathetic little face. I made him take out what he was hiding.

My friends, what do you suppose it was? Just a bit of the white paper, which had been lost from the cap of one of the babies and which he had put away because it smelled of perfume. Do you wonder that I wanted to take that little fellow on my knee and give him some of the things for which he craved and which the drab life of a country at war denied him? He was allowed to keep his treasure without further stigma.

Surely no piece of wrapping-paper ever served such a triple purpose before,—first a table-cloth, then a cap, and finally a treasure hoarded by a small boy because it smelled *bon*—good.

I wrote that story to a friend of mine who taught on the east side of New York. She read it to her class. They put their heads together and decided to send some crackers to the babies who had none. Meanwhile war restrictions on sending packages overseas had gone into effect. So the boxes and boxes of crackers which they brought to school were sent to hospital children at home. But the class was not satisfied. Something must be done for French children. So the girls made duster bags and peddled them from house to house until they had earned thirteen dollars to send to me for buying more crackers for my charges. I managed to get a few, through a nurse who had a vacation in England, for it was well-nigh impossible to obtain them in France. The rest of the money was spent in buying phonograph records, of the need for which I have already spoken. I felt that it was the best way in which I could carry out the wishes of that east-side class. I left it to the judgment of the clerk who called upon me, to choose French records for me. The choice proved to be such a success in our hospital that we decided to give a village entertainment. Having nothing better than a baby carriage in which to wheel down the phonograph, we felt something like circus performers as we wended our way through the one village street, flanked on each side by curious onlookers. We were well repaid, however, for we had to repeat the performance three or four times.

Then there came the sad day of parting forever from the work which held me in a grip that has never loosened. We gave a good-bye entertainment, and by that time I was able to speak enough French to tell the audience of the message of love from the little east-side children who had helped to buy the records. The message went straight home to the hearts of the French. Even the soldiers, some of whom were always quartered at Bettancourt ready to be sent at a moment's notice to either front, accustomed though they were to the hardships of war, had tears in their eyes as they whispered with bated breath, " The little Americans did that for our children. The little, little Americans—the little Americans." That east-side class had formed invisible ties of friendship.

IX

ARMISTICE DAY AND AFTER

James A. Norton served under the Quakers in France, Germany, and elsewhere in Europe in relief work during and after the war. Both during the war and afterward he made trips for the inspection of work and of possible fields for work. He is therefore well posted on what were the needs of Europe. He saw the common people of many countries, and came back filled with the desire of working for a better world. He has had experience as a newspaper reporter, as secretary to a Congressman, and as manager of a travel bureau. Now he is in the financial department of a large manufacturing company.

WHEN asked to give reminiscences of work in France with the Quaker Reconstruction Unit, I think of the eleventh hour of the morning of the eleventh day of the eleventh month, 1918—can anyone who was in Paris on that fateful day and hour ever forget?

For days the negotiations for an armistice had been going on in Marshal Foch's private car at the front. The terms had been laid down. The time limit for an answer had been named. What was before us?

The morning papers told us that if the terms were accepted and the armistice signed, that fact would be announced by the firing of guns and the blowing of sirens—both grim reminders of the nights of the air

80

raids, now happily a thing of the past—or were they? And eleven o'clock was to be the time.

" Business as usual " seemed descriptive of Paris as the morning hours wore on. The day was fair and mild, with just a suggestion of haze in the air. People went about their business and their work as though nothing eventful was taking place. But as the clock hands passed ten, there came a little tension, men and women were looking at clocks and watches, wondering —listening.

And then it drew on toward eleven. My own duties of the day called me into a southern working-class quarter of the city, where I went to obtain from a small factory some working parts for one of our trucks, whose obstinacy rivalled that of the proverbial army mule, and added measurably to the horrors of war.

France was at war, but the appearance of that working-class quarter seemed peaceful enough. The broad, sunny streets, pleasant with small trees, were swept and clean—cleaner, I dare say, than many streets in New York or Philadelphia. The sidewalks had been brushed, the once whitewashed stone houses still all but gleamed in the sun. All was quiet and serene—indeed, the very quiet and serenity were mute witnesses of the state of the nation, for there was a notable absence of men in street and shop, and only an occasional vehicle in the street.

Then, when the church clock chimed the three-quarters, and the hands moved toward ten minutes of the hour, the street began to take on more animation.

Doors opened, women, old, middle-aged, young, appeared on door-stoops. Here and there, in shop doors, a man, but mostly women without their men. At first there was a little chatter from door to door, light comments on weather and health, which little betrayed what was on their minds.

Now the clock had passed five minutes of the hour, and a hush fell upon the street, an air of expectancy, while the women looked up and listened. The anxiety of their faces now showed clearly enough what they were thinking, these women folk of French working men—would they sign? Was the four years of horror over, or must it go on?

The clock began to strike, one, no other sound; two, no other sound, and so on to seven or eight, and some faces were turned sorrowfully houseward. But hark! What was that? A gun, from the direction of the Seine! Then another and another and another, and the sirens, from Nôtre Dame and many another tower, until all Paris was filled with the noise—noises which had been terrible enough when they bespoke air raids, but which brought quite another message now.

" *C'est la Paix! C'est la Paix!* " " It is Peace! It is Peace! " cried the women of that Paris working quarter. They embraced, they wept, they laughed all at once. The few men shook hands and smiled, albeit a little tearfully. The scene was a most moving one. And its keynote that first cry, " *C'est la Paix!* "

An hour later, back in the Place de la Concorde, the newsboys were crying special editions which carried broad headlines, clear across the page, " *C'est la*

Victoire." " It is victory." Paris went wild. Trucks
chased about the streets, going nowhere as fast as they
could, blowing their horns and carrying shouting, arm-
waving men and women, boys and girls. Old and
young danced in the streets. The cafés were crowded.
From eleven in the morning until nearly the next
morning the city was frantic with joy and excitement.
" *C'est la Victoire, c'est la Victoire,*" was the cry. But
through it all, and on every eleventh of November
since, my memory has gone back to the cry of those
working women of France: " *C'est la Paix!* "

With peace came greater opportunities for the
Quaker Unit to go on with the work of relief and reconstruction it had carried on during the war.

There was not a civilian in Varennes when the first
two Quaker relief workers arrived. Two brave girls,
they were, one from America and the other from
England, and both caring more about helping people
than about their own comfort. There was not a house
fit for human habitation, either, and, deep with mud,
with the rain still pouring down, Varennes looked and
was a desolate waste. But back in undevastated
France were families anxious to get to their homes, for
though the houses were gone, the land was still home
to them. Months and years of work lay before them
in restoring their pleasant town.

These two brave girls came and opened up the town,
settling in a German dugout—timbered in front, the
earth above supported by elephant iron; they had a
military cemetery for their front yard. The truck
occasionally coming from the Quaker centre ten miles

away was their only link with civilization. The truck brought to them cans of milk, cans of beef and bags of flour, bales of goods, partly worn and cheap new clothing, medical supplies, garden tools, and carpenters' tools—the means of making rude but useful furniture.

They were there to welcome the first French family that returned to the town, and they made it a home until its members could put up a hut for themselves. They got in touch with the mayor of Varennes and through him with the citizens of the town who wished to return, and helped them to do so.

At night the rats would run through their dugout, and even across their beds. One morning they awoke to find coloured American soldiers removing the bodies from the cemetery which was their front lawn, for orders had come from headquarters to move all bodies of American soldiers to the great central military cemeteries. Another morning a hand grenade or un-exploded small shell got into the fire with the kindling. When it went off it plastered the walls of the dugout with oatmeal.

Gradually civilization rolled up about them. Transportation came in the shape of horses and then a light truck and finally Jerry—of whom I shall tell you more later. Soon they had also a portable house, where they could live, from which they could distribute their supplies, and in which they could receive the returning refugees. The population of the surrounding country began to increase; Varennes became the seat of a medical centre and Quaker hospital, a co-operative store, a transportation unit. Varennes itself and the nearby villages, places like Montfaucon and other landmarks of the American advance, had Quaker building units constructing portable houses for the returning refugees. Once they built as many as four houses in one village in a single day. The place was a scene of humming constructive activity, in sharp contrast to the destruction of the year before and the desolation of the winter.

The two girls are now at home, one in America and one in England. The men of the Quaker unit who aided them and followed them with buildings, stores, farm implements and animals, also went back to their homes. The people of Varennes, and the other villages about, settled down to the long pull of permanent reconstruction in stone. But they had the advantage of settling down to their task in wooden houses which the Quakers from England and America had built for them, and with tools, materials, seeds and implements these Quakers had brought them. And always the honour of opening up Varennes to civilian habitation after the war will belong to those two brave Quaker girls who lived in an elephant-iron German dugout behind a cemetery where lay American boys who had given their lives to end war.

Jerry, of whom I spoke, was neither man nor beast, yet he was one of the most useful members ever added to the Quaker Relief Unit in France. One of the young American relief workers, otherwise known as a Young Yank, moved by curiosity to explore the waste lands around the Meuse-Argonne battlefield, discovered Jerry sitting on the siding of an abandoned military railroad, and investigated. Jerry was a big

German auto truck, fitted with flanged wheels to run on rails, a motor specially equipped for pulling freight cars, and geared to go at the same speed forward and backward. He was promptly christened Jerry, partly in honour of the sturdy prisoners of war from over the Rhine who toiled with us in erecting houses for the returned refugees, and with our neighbours the French peasants, in filling in trenches and removing barbed wire. The name was appropriate, and it stuck.

Jerry was not immediately useful. It had been six months since his creator, the German army, had moved back beyond the hills of Vauquois and La Fille Morte, in the Argonne scenes of unforgetable devastation, and Jerry had stood out through a wet French winter. But the transport department of our unit had tackled and tamed everything from a Ford motor to a Rolls Royce, including Dodges, Liberties, Sunbeams, Fiats, Daimlers, Panhards, and the best products of three automobile-using nations, so a motor of a fourth nationality looked interesting but not insurmountable. Jerry was towed to the machine shop at Grange-le-Comte, and almost before the rest of us had heard of his existence, the trial run was announced. The first run of a steam railroad train on the Baltimore and Ohio Railroad a hundred years ago was not a more momentous event to Baltimore or Ohio than was Jerry's first run in 1919 to our little group. And he worked!

And how he did work in the days that followed! There were carloads of supplies to be brought over on our long siding from Clermont. The railroad yard at

Aubreville, where sections of portable houses had been unloaded to be hauled by trucks up to Varennes and beyond to furnish human habitation where there was none (an abandoned dugout hardly deserves the name of human habitation)—this unloading station now became a switching station, and small trainloads of our sectional houses followed Jerry up over the thirty-mile railroad the American army had so obligingly left. Then there were provisions and supplies to go into the co-operative store at Varennes, and goats, chickens and cows to go to the farmers there and farther north, in a country that had been stripped clean by the passage of two armies, fighting as they passed. If Jerry had helped to bring up the implements of destruction, he was now turned to bringing the means of reconstruction. He covered a run of about thirty miles.

So great was the task, however, that Jerry needed help, as soon became very evident. What was to be done? The Germans were gone, far away. There was no other vehicle of the kind in France, so far as we knew. But the transport department was not stumped. If German trucks could be made to run on rails, why not American trucks? So one of the big Liberties was taken off the road and put on the rails with flanged rear wheels and the front wheels mounted on a little hand-car. But the Liberty had to turn around for the return trip, and that means a turn-table at each end of the line. So turn-tables were provided.

Now the private railroad was in full operation, and as transport of new materials is of vital importance in a devastated country, in the area where Jerry and the

Liberty worked and the boys who ran them and handled the supplies they brought, reconstruction went on at a pace that surprised all visitors. The Meuse will be years recovering from the war, but perhaps it will not be quite so many years as it would have been without the Quaker-manned Jerry.

X

STILL IN FRANCE AFTER THE WAR

ALFRED LOWRY *was a teacher before he went to Paris with his family to become head of the important Quaker centre there.*

Through this centre pass many Quaker workers and pleasure travellers, so it has a broader touch with the world than have the other centres in Berlin, Warsaw, Vienna or elsewhere. It is the purpose of these centres to be embassies of good will to the people of the countries where they are located. The Quakers hope, some day, to have a chain of such centres over the world, where will dwell self-supporting men and women, living examples of good will to the world around them.

A YOUNG Frenchman whom I admire and respect comes occasionally to our Quaker office in Paris. The war cost him both his eyes, and also his right arm. He holds out no pencils at a street corner, but earns his living as a telephone operator. One day some one in the office was commiserating with him, lamenting over the horrible plight in which the Germans had left him. He protested at once: " We must not hate the Germans; we must only hate war! "

That spirit illustrates what we are working for, in the Quaker international centres in Europe. It is about these centres that I want to speak now.

As a result of the Quaker reconstruction work in

the devastated areas of France, the refugee work in Poland, the daily feeding of 1,000,000 school children in Germany and the anti-tuberculosis campaign and land settlement in Austria, a widespread interest was aroused in the Quaker work. It was in response to this interest that the British and American Quakers founded the chain of international good-will centres which now stretches from Paris to Warsaw, and even Moscow, and includes besides these three cities, London, Geneva, Rome, Berlin, Vienna, and Salonika.

The French are a peace-loving people. I have lived among them for six years in all, mostly in the heart of Paris. All they ask for is security—to live their lives, earn their living, bring up their families. The Germans, also, are a peaceable people. I have lived amongst them, too, at intervals. What they, also, ask for is security. I am sure that other peoples, amongst whom I have not lived, are also peace-loving peoples who, like the French and the Germans, must be *goaded* into war, and who ask only for security.

How is this security obtainable? It is the task of our Quaker centres to convince people that international security is to be had much more certainly, and much more cheaply, by the policies of friendliness, openness, and active good will than by the old methods —which never work—of distrust, force of arms and war. We seek to build up a spirit of understanding.

At our Paris centre, for example, to take the one I know most about, we have a book shop, where are sold books and pamphlets which we ourselves publish or which are published by others, dealing with all sorts of international and economic problems. We issue a paper, called *L'Echo des Amis,* which goes not only to many parts of France, but to French-speaking Belgium, Switzerland, the colonies of Algeria, Indo-China and New Caledonia (two months away in the South Seas), and to the Balkan countries, where many people understand French.

We organize lectures by eminent speakers, and we ourselves give addresses, when opportunity offers, before other groups and movements in Paris or the provinces, sometimes as far away as the south of France.   Each Quaker centre serves as a clearinghouse of information about one country to another, by keeping in constant touch with the Quaker centres in the other countries, including, of course, America and England.   We are able to reply to many sorts of inquiries by individuals or groups in our country who are seeking information about conditions in another country.   A young Japanese, now in the diplomatic service, came to us in Paris for help with the thesis he was preparing for his doctor's degree.   We were able to give the help he needed.   Later, when he departed for Tokyo, we gave him the address of our Quaker headquarters in Japan, that he might keep in touch with our work in his own country.

We maintain contacts with many movements and like-minded groups in France.   When the " Jeune Republique "—a peace movement among young Catholics under the magnetic leadership of Marc Sangnier, a former member of the Chamber of Deputies—was getting ready for its great peace congress in 1926, at

Bierville, near Paris (at which 6,000 people were in attendance, about one-half of them Germans), two of our group were asked to serve on the organization committee.

Foreigners who, for one reason or another, have become stranded in Paris, frequently apply to us for help. Sometimes they think we are " easy marks," and demand absurdly extravagant things. Like the man who wanted a ticket from Paris to Havana, Cuba —probably for other reasons than those which today attract to Havana the average American tourist! But some of these stranded people whom we have been able to help would probably have been able to find help nowhere else.

Our work includes the interpretation of France to American and other visitors—helping to make their stay more agreeable and worth while, that they may return home with a better understanding of the real France and the French people. I stress this word, *understanding*, which is the basis of all our effort. A French proverb says that to understand all is to forgive all (one cannot hate a people whom one has come to understand).

At times this service to Americans or others takes very simple, concrete form—meeting people at the trains, getting hotel accommodations, supplying information about schools, finding families with whom they can live, helping them to plan their stay and to do and see the things that they will find most worth while and interesting. When people do not speak the French language, and their time in France is limited, such help often reveals to them a France they had not dreamed of. We shall welcome *you* when you come to Paris if you will let us know in advance, or look us up when you get there. Our office is now at 12 rue Guy de la Brosse, on the left bank of the Seine, near the University Clubs, which have played an important rôle in our work among the cosmopolitan population of students in Geneva, Frankfurt, Berlin, and Vienna. Student clubs have played an important rôle in the work of the Quaker centres. We in Paris hope to establish such clubs there.

Before I conclude, I want to tell you a little about our work for foreign and other prisoners. France— progressive in many lines—seems almost mediæval in her prisons.

Thanks to the efforts of two devoted women, members of our Quaker staff, one Dutch and the other a Pole, many unfortunate foreign girls and women in two Paris prisons were helped. These two women spoke seven languages between them: Russian, Polish, Dutch, French, German, English, Italian. They acted as interpreters in the court-room, visited the girls in prison (some of them had no clear idea why they were there), and helped them after their release—either to find work in France or, if they were under sentence of deportation, to come in contact with persons in their own country, if possible through another Quaker centre, who would take an interest in them.

A French prison reform committee was organized by the Quakers. The dean of the Law School of the University of Paris is a member of this committee.

The latter has effected the transfer of a large number of women from the indescribably bad prisons of St. Lazare to the much more modern one of Fresnes, outside of Paris. The committee has also been able to secure authorization for holding occasional concerts by some of the most eminent French musicians, in prisons for men, women, boys and girls. Many of these prisoners have been much touched—as is evidenced by their letters—by this demonstration of interest in their welfare. A member of the committee, who is also a member of our Quaker group, has been appointed a probation officer, and he also has broadcastings over the radio every Saturday evening, on aspects of penal reform. He has spoken in favour of the abolition of the death penalty, and has described model penal institutions in Belgium and Switzerland.

Our international Quaker centres do not seek to turn people into Quakers. Yet we find everywhere people in close sympathy with our point of view and our work. Often groups of sympathizers find in the Quaker centres a spiritual home. In Paris, amongst a gathering of thirty-five people at our Quaker centre, I have counted as many as twelve nationalities —including Egyptian and Chinese. This, in itself, is an opportunity for adventures in international understanding.

No one wants war, and rarely is any one to be found who believes in war. But negative belief is not enough.

There is no sentence in the Bible, " Blessed are those who do not believe in war." There *is* a sentence among the recorded sayings of Jesus, " Blessed are those who *make peace!* " It is in an effort to make for peace by building up a spirit of understanding and good will that the Quaker international centres are engaged.

XI

FEEDING A MILLION CHILDREN

FRIEDA M. BURKLE *is a dietician by training who went to Germany after the war to help in the work of child-feeding. Her friends say that she was the real author of the cookbook which guided the feeding of over a million children a day in Germany during the time of greatest need. She has been to South America seeking to aid people through her profession, and now lives and feeds people in the heart of the city of New York.*

MOST of us would think a family of fifty a large family. When I served the noonday meal to seven hundred school children in Boston, Massachusetts, it seemed to me that we were cooking food in large quantities. But in July, 1920, in the city of Essen, Germany, I found Fraulein Wolf and her co-workers preparing the daily meal for twenty thousand mothers and children. This was large-scale cookery. Later on I saw kitchens in which thirty-three thousand and thirty-five thousand meals were prepared at one time, but they never impressed me as being quite so stupendous as this kitchen in the stock-yards of Essen, the city where the great Krupp steel works are located.

In German the word Essen means " to eat," and it also means " chimneys." The towering brick chimneys of Essen, standing black against the horizon, form as impressive a picture as the sky-line of New York. But they looked sinister to me in their black majesty. There was no smoke issuing from their mouths. That meant that there was no work to do, and idle hands meant less food to eat for those who were already hungry. The stock-yard seemed a fitting place to prepare the food for the thousands of under-nourished children and mothers. The immense space, the high kettles, the empty stalls where animals should have been, the silence of the place, all bore mute testimony to the activity of other days and the need now for more food than could be found in this thickly settled industrial area of the Ruhr.

In this district, in 1921, the Quakers were feeding two hundred and fifty thousand women and children.

The soup was cooked by steam in six six-hundred-quart kettles. Work began at one in the morning, and by seven o'clock the bread was cut and in the baskets, the soup was in fifty-quart thermos kettles ready for the street-cars bearing the legend, " Quaker *speisung* " (Quaker feeding), to carry it to the nearest points for the feeding centres, to which nursing and expectant mothers, and children from two to seventeen years of age, came at ten o'clock in the morning, or at four in the afternoon, for a piece of bread and a bowl of soup.

This daily meal they received only on the recommendation of the municipal physician. For this purpose they were examined by physicians and if found to be in serious need—and " serious " meant marked evidence of undernourishment—they were given a card which admitted them to the feeding each day. They paid from 25 to 40 pfennigs if they could afford it; if not, the food was given free. This sum was paid to the community to cover the cost of the fuel and transportation. Those in charge of the cooking were for the most part volunteers. There were forty thousand workers. The German government provided all the sugar and flour that was needed for the Quaker feeding as soon as it was able to do so. This was from October, 1920, on.

Perhaps you have never seen children who have been hungry for a long time—not just an hour or a day, but months and years. You will find it hard to picture the stunted children, so dwarfed by lack of food that twelve-year-olds looked eight years old, to eyes unaccustomed to famine scenes. It would be unpleasant to dwell on the fact that the elongated heads of so many of the children, the curious swaying walk and the misshapen arms and legs, resulting from softening of the bones, were due to lack of food. So great was the shortage of fats that I often saw children weeping bitterly because they could have no more cod-liver oil. Our supply of this oil never met more than two per cent of the need, yet cod-liver oil came to us by the barrel in ship-loads.

Imagine these groups of fifty, one hundred or five hundred or a thousand children " Quakering," as it was called; eating their bean-soup, or rice-soup or cocoa and roll—some of them eating it fast, in the hope that there might be a little more left because Hans or Mariechen was absent; others using their fingers to scrape out the last drop of the cocoa or rice (these

were the favourite dishes), and occasionally others
making it last longer by eating as slowly as possible.
One little fellow wanted for his birthday, his seventh,
a piece of bread as big as the one the mothers got.
The day's ration for children from six to fourteen years
averaged six hundred and sixty calories; that is about
equal to two eggs and an equal amount each of bread
and beans.   Mothers received about half as much
again, and the younger children half of what the
ten-year-olds had.

In one kitchen—it was a basement room, the walls
were whitewashed, and on each table, white from
scrubbing, was an empty red-labelled evaporated milk
can holding sprigs of evergreen, such a cheery room!—
I found the children eating soup made of beans and
cocoa cooked together.   There was a misprint in the
menu, it read, " Beans and cocoa soup," instead of
" Beans or cocoa soup."   It was not a favourite dish,
but the children ate it willingly, for they were hungry.

In order to see whether we could improve the bread
that we were using, I baked a few sample rolls and
took the specimens home with me to the children in
the family where I was living.   The five-year-old son
was so delighted to have the white roll that he wanted
to keep it; he had never seen such white bread.

The first book or collection of recipes, menus and
directions for the " Quaker Kitchens " was prepared,
before I arrived in Germany, by Fraulein Audrussov
with the aid and advice of leading dietitians and physicians in Berlin.   The food materials were fat, sugar,
evaporated milk, cocoa, rice, beans and flour; these

are concentrated foods, which could stand being transported and could be stored for a long time.

Questions, of course, came up from time to time about the materials and the recipes. If they could not be settled through correspondence I would visit the kitchen to see what could be done. At one time reports came from the district offices that the flour was not thickening the soup, and the rolls were not so big as they ought to be; on analysis it was found that the wheat had been cut while still green, the flour therefore contained more than thirteen per cent water. By keeping it in a warm place and allowing a certain weight for the water that dried out, the soup and rolls were again of the right thickness and size. Such a matter was serious, for it affected over four thousand kitchens preparing seven hundred thousand meals daily and using four hundred and eight grams (about one pound) of flour for each child a week.

Again, reports came from the districts that the rice contained bird seed; this turned out to be grains of wild rice mixed with the other, and when it was understood the problem was solved. Another time from a little village in the Vogtland we received word that the children had been made ill from eating the bean-soup. On investigation it turned out that several bags of those beans had fallen into the salt water on loading or unloading from the ship, they became mouldy and should not have been used. They were discarded and allowance made for the loss. In another place boxes which should have contained cocoa were found to be filled to the exact weight with scrap-iron. However, dishonesty or thieving of any kind was extremely rare. I am told that this scrap-iron was wedged together with newspapers printed in Trenton, New Jersey.

In order to discuss common problems in regard to the cooking and serving of the food, I held conferences in Munich, Dresden, Leipzig, Hamburg, Cologne, Coblenz, Mainz, Prinasens and Beuthen with groups ranging from fifty to two hundred people at a time.

From 1920 to 1922 I revised the cook-book four times. This was due to changes in our food materials; *i. e.*, sweetened condensed milk was used for a time instead of lard, and finally during the summer months the ration was changed, allowing more milk and less fat. Every effort was made to adjust the food to the psychological and physical needs of the time and place. For instance, in Hamburg sweet soups were served. In the Leipzig district a thick cocoa-soup, in Beuthen a rice-soup without milk.

In the conferences with workers from all parts of Germany, I was impressed over and over again with the deep understanding of what the Quakers tried to express in their work, in the co-operation which they extended to us on all sides and in the spirit in which they carried on their work. They, too, many of them volunteers working from one and two o'clock in the morning to prepare the food for their charges, showed their faith and good will toward men.

Sometimes as the hosts of children stood to thank me, and through me America and those who made it possible for them to have the food they had received, I wondered: What will be the result of all this in the

minds of these little ones when they are grown? And
I remembered the little boy whom I asked if he liked
chocolate as he stood looking longingly at a window
display of candy. He answered: " Every man loves
chocolate." After he had picked out what he wanted
—I think it cost one mark, just a few cents—his eyes
beamed, he thanked me with his whole little body, and
rushed off to share it with others. I believe this
gesture of good will toward women and children in sore
distress will return not only to America but to the
whole world, the measure " heaped up, pressed down
and running over," when these little ones take up the
problems we leave for them to inherit and carry on.

XII

FIGHTING FAMINE

NANCY J. BABB, *who came from lower Virginia, has had much social service experience in America. She was one of the Quaker workers who went to the valley of the Volga in 1917, and since then has spent a large part of her time in Russia. She took the first train load of supplies into Samara Province in the autumn of 1921, following the summer when less rain fell there than fell in the Sahara Desert. Before long she was stricken with typhus fever. She begins her story after her recovery from typhus.*

The fame of her helpfulness and efficiency spread so widely that the people of one of the other provinces of Russia sent her a letter of invitation, reading, " Come thou, Nancy, and rule over us."

AFTER the summer of 1921, when there was less rain in the valley of the Russian Volga than in the desert of Sahara, when people were collecting leaves and straw for their winter food, I went with the first train-load of food supplies to the Buzuluk district, where the Quakers eventually clothed and fed half a million famine victims a day.

My work was interrupted by an attack of typhus fever, but after my recovery, in December, I went out to the village of Totskoy, fifty miles from Buzuluk city and about a thousand miles southeast of Moscow, to help the peasant committees distribute the car-loads

103

of Quaker clothing and food. This included such articles as flour, cocoa, sugar, lard, salt fish; grains, corn, canned foods, cod-liver oil; and frozen carcasses of Australian meat, which might have been carcasses of rhinoceroses, wild buffalo or anything of the sort, judging from the size. Clothing of all sorts, shapes, forms and sizes, and suitable for all sorts of occasions, were included in the bales of clothing. Everything was needed and usable except the ball-room slippers and peek-a-boo blouses.

Over each door of our warehouses and offices we had posted the Quaker stars well known by their four black points, alternating with their four red smaller points.

The day's journey on seven sledges took us to this village, where accommodations had not yet been prepared for us in spite of the telegrams and orders from the government to prepare suitable quarters. Like real refugees we stored our supplies in the one lockable room recommended by the postmaster, and for the first night slept on our trunks, tables and chairs in what was to be our future office.

The next morning my one American companion, with her interpreter, went away, leaving me alone and with no passport, in this village of eleven hundred, to organize the Quaker relief work for forty-three villages covering an area of three thousand square miles with sixty-three thousand population. Many were already dying of starvation and freezing for the want of the clothes which they had sold to buy food to keep them alive up to this time.

This village of Totskoy, though centrally located

and the political headquarters for the district, was three miles from the station and had no warehouses suitable to accommodate our supplies. These we were compelled to store, during the first year, at the station in care of the government, the Quakers holding the keys while the government had to be present each morning when the seals were broken. Rather dreading the daily cold drive through blizzards to this station and fearing being lost in the storms, and having my face frozen frequently, I wanted to live at the station, but the good-natured official assured me that the Quakers really should not settle at the lonely station. After looking around all one day, finally they found me a four-room tiny, one-story peasant cottage which had been nationalized by the government and had been recently occupied by seven families, including one typhus case.

This was my new home in Totskoy, a typical Russian village, where I was destined to work in various forms of Quaker relief for the next six years. What a warm welcome! Though the seven families had willingly departed, they had left active little friends hiding under the torn wall paper, in the cracks of the floors and all over the springless iron bedsteads. The vermin were little disturbed by the slamming blinds, rag-stuffed windows, falling doors and torn dusty wall paper. The six hungry government workers employed to clean up, having made little headway in four days, I released them, and with two women to help me I took the necessary steps, after office hours the next day, to make the little hut clean and habitable.

All the soap in our personal baggage, all the lysol and crude carbolic solution, was poured into iron kettles of boiling water. With an improvised mop made by tying a rag to the end of a stick, I soon put an end to the millions of bugs hiding in the beds, under the wall paper and in the floor crevices. With chalk from the native hills ground into powder, an old-fashioned whitewash was made, and a liberal coat given to the interior of the walls and ceilings. This treatment made the little cottage at least clean, though another week passed before the general repairs were finished, and this turmoil was after we had moved in from our refugee quarters.

I was told that my house was on the famous Bandit Row, but the kind-hearted Russo-Japenese army cook, now a Russian government official, begged me not to fear the bandits, as the twenty Communists already killed and buried on my street would prove to have been the last to perish. In a few days the government was going to send a whole battalion of soldiers to defend the town, and some of these were going to be quartered in my little cottage for my protection. A week after we had organized the feeding, five hundred people arrived in front of our house. The warehouse man's wife became hysterical, Andy turned pale with fright. The cook ran up the ladder to the top of the stove—like all Russian stoves, a sort of tiled wardrobe-like box. Tonya, the warehouse man's wife, shrieked, saying that she was going to leave immediately, whether her husband went or not. A rap on the door, quickly followed by a second rap, announced that some one had arrived with demands. I opened and, sure enough, there stood a large group of men. " Who are you, and on what authority have you come here? " I asked kindly. They replied calmly, pointing to their rifles:

" We are Soviet soldiers from the Red Army sent to defend the town against bandits. Please give us quarters here, so we can look out for your personal protection."

I told them that we were Quakers and did not need the protection of arms nor did we fear the bandits. They looked amazed. They were a lot of men, mostly very dirty and evidently hungry. Giving them each a loaf of bread, I asked them to leave me alone. I was very busy with the food committees. Moreover, they would find all our houses marked with the Quaker stars, and at such places their services would not be needed.

The next day the head of the village soviet, the governing committee, was astonished on hearing the story. He was surprised to find us without armed protection; he, being a Communist, very much questioned the wisdom, and all the more when he found me without a passport.

Tonya, Andy and Eleanna all informed me that unless I conformed to the rules and allowed the soldiers to remain for protection they would have to leave me. To this I replied, " Go where you feel comfortable, but I shall remain here." Then they began to become more calm.

In a few days bandits came to the village where our

food supplies were housed, but the committees, not wishing to disturb me, met the bandits themselves, explained the stars and that the Quakers were feeding little children especially, all regardless of race, creed or party affiliations. The bandits looked at the food and forbade their men to take any, but took all the soviet horses, made the wife of the Communist kill their one cow to feed them, and departed, saying they would return shortly. The bandits did return, according to their promise, both a second time and a third time. The second time they took nothing. The third time they explained that they could not go on without food enough to reach the next village, so this time they took food for a single meal apiece—less than a guard of soldiers would have eaten in a single day. Again they said we would see them once more, but they never had the face to return the fourth time after taking even those few mouthfuls of food that had been meant for children.

Neither tongue nor pen can portray the awful conditions which existed at this time among the peasants. Teachers were almost ready to faint from hunger, other teachers in remote districts were digging the graves of teachers who had died of starvation. The unburied dead were lying on all sides, stripped of the last vestige of clothing because there was not enough clothing left to cover the living.

It is a soul-harrowing experience to be comfortably housed in a warm cottage, with adequate food, and to be helpless when you hear children outside crying for bread, and nearly naked. Yet even if you know you might find them lying starved and frozen on your door-step in the morning, you must not feed them, because there is too little food for all. If you do not keep yourself an efficient worker, the whole feeding system will break down and many others will die because you are short-sighted.

Food and reports were so inadequate that I had to visit the feeding stations repeatedly to supervise the distribution of the food. In the worst of the famine the chief of the village soviet wanted to send soldiers to protect me for fear that the horse might be killed for food in some villages I visited. Without soldiers, I started out. This displeased the owner of the horse and sleigh, who had expected soldiers to accompany us. So, after having gone through two villages with me, the driver became so much frightened that he refused to continue the journey, leaving me twenty-five miles from home and thirty miles to the distant villages. I secured another driver, who had the only swift horse in the village. He took me forty miles over the steppes to several Tartar villages, saying that with that horse he was afraid of neither the wolves nor the Tartars.

The driver was so busy asking about America and the Quakers that he paid little attention to his large dog, which was constantly chasing wolf after wolf from the beaten track.

At the first one of these villages the Mohammedan mullah from the church steeple was calling the people to noon-day prayers, while across the road a soldier guarded the open common grave. The policeman who was in charge of the distribution, the only Russian-speaking man of the village, expressed his gratitude to the Quakers, as tears trickled down his cheeks. At the next village the mullah was in charge. His books were in order, and he said as we started off, " How dared you come alone, and what can all this generosity mean? Has God not forgotten us? " At that very moment, from the village across the broad expanse of the white steppes, could be seen the sunset more gorgeous than pen or brush can paint. " One God, and the brotherhood of man," I said. Had I made it clear?

The impatient driver snapped his whip, and soon we were miles from the Mohammedan mullah, whom we left facing this sunset.

As soon as the winter was over a reconstruction program was organized in co-operation with the local government. Who wished for food had to work! This led to the rapid organization of inspectors of labour of many kinds, who co-operated with my central committees in seeing that the roads were staked out or repaired, orphanages provided, adult schools organized, furniture made, schools repaired, medical stations repaired, club houses, public halls and libraries repaired, home industries established—such as embroidery and weaving, farm buildings repaired, land ploughed for those who had lost their horses in the famine, hay cut, bridges built, plague exterminations undertaken, typhus barracks arranged, or built, to care for the many sufferers, and countless other activities too numerous to mention. By this time the improved weather was speeding up transportation from the outside world, so food and clothing was now available sufficient to pay for all work done.

The third phase of our work—medical relief and medical instruction—naturally followed, for many were unable to work. Mothers knew little about the use of foreign food. Also, as food became less needed, though more scarce in some places, it was necessary to decide by doctors' inspections who were entitled to this assistance. Especially was this true when the malaria epidemics followed the famine. Often seventy-five per cent of a village were afflicted with some form of malaria, and every one was anxious to get a bit of the precious quinine, whether actually ill or not.

A group of doctors and nurses were organized for this work, out of which were finally selected the better ones for our permanent health centre and child welfare work at Totskoy, Sorochenskoye and Buzuluk. All of this work has now been adopted as a part of the government program, and is supported by the government.

Near Totskoy, and connected with Totskoy work, a sanatorium of one hundred and twenty-five children's beds was reconstructed, equipped and supported by the Quakers for three years, after which it also was turned over to the government. So also were the farms totalling eight hundred and fifty acres. These farms had been turned over to the Quakers for large-scale farming and were cultivated by tractors, mostly, and used chiefly for food supplies for the hospital and sanatorium.

As the government had promised eventually to take over this work, it seemed advisable for them to do so.

They in turn urged us to use the funds from the liqui-
dation and salvage supplies for the construction of an
additional fireproof brick hospital, which they would
supplement should the Quaker funds be insufficient to
actually complete the hospital. A part of the funds
had already been used to equip the sanatorium for
summer patients, but I finally agreed to undertake the
work if the local government would authorize the sale
of supplies without license and would make up the
deficit. They agreed. Machinery, even second-hand
machinery, had such a highly artificial value here, so
far from civilization, that converting it into cash and
the cash into a hospital seemed possible.

Though it proved more expensive and complicated
than anticipated, the hospital was finally completed
fourteen months after date agreed—and this in spite
of floods, fires, labour union strikers, thefts, delays
and a score of other complications and disappointments. Bricks, the first since the war, were made on
the premises, lumber was hauled from the forest one
hundred miles away, and skilled labour ordered from
the near-by cities, while such things as glass, medical
instruments, and plumbing equipment were ordered
from Moscow and Germany. The local government
made up the deficit of $4,000 and supervised the final
construction of this thirty-bed village hospital and
medical centre, just in time for dedication at the tenth
anniversary of the Russian revolution. It is now being
supported by the government. It fills an urgent need
and is always busy, having an out-patient dispensary,
a drug store, a clinic for mothers and tuberculosis

work, providing weekly health lectures in the schools, and arranging mothers' meetings. The latter are illustrated with pictures—the first thing of the kind in the village.

This hospital has the best rural medical service available in Russia, but, like all other hospitals of Russia, it is in need of the professionally trained nurse who does not exist in all Russia. This lack accounts for the high death rate in many departments of Russia's health work.

Just as the Quakers have always made it a principle to be most economical in the use of funds and overhead expenses, they have likewise sought out fields of service most needed and so far untouched, fields which seem to mean the most in the way of real help to Russia. The organization of a Nurses' Training School is today a field of service unfilled by any agency and a field in which the Russian government welcomes assistance and co-operation.

XIII

ACROSS THE STEPPES OF RUSSIA

ANNA J. HAINES *is an American Quaker who has been in Russia much of the time for the past ten years. The interest of Quakers in Russia began when Peter the Great attended a Quaker meeting in London. Under the Czars Quakers frequently went to Russia, one of the most prominent being William Allen, the partner of Robert Owen, who visited the country a hundred years ago. So under the government of the last of the Czars the English Quakers sent out workers to Russia early in the war. Anna J. Haines followed these. She was the first person sent down to Samara Province in 1921, when rumours of famine reached the Quakers. What she says of Russia comes from one so impressed with the needs of humanity that she came back to America and took a complete training as nurse. Then she returned there, to do what she could for the people.*

I AM a Quaker nurse and my particular part in Quaker adventuring has been the search for health and its defense, a pursuit which offered plenty of adventures when our unit first went out, in the war days of 1917. My life was by no means tame in the famine days of 1921, and on my last visit to Russia, a year ago, adventures still kept turning up.

Our first entrance into Russia—at the railroad station of Vladivostok, while Kerensky was still in power —brought us some of our problems. Hundreds of dirty refugees, old men in evil-smelling sheepskin

coats, women in trailing skirts, children whose torn
rags showed their vermin-scarred little bodies, bony
babies sometimes wrapped only in newspapers, lay or
crawled around the greasy floors of the big station.
Whatever of household goods they could carry—bundles, wooden chests, unpolished samovars—were huddled at each family's feet. Only by stepping on these
lumpy impediments could one avoid trampling on
human beings. Most of these refugees had been driven
from their homes in Poland, five thousand miles away,
by the advancing German army, and were piling up
at the Pacific seaboard because the freight cars in
which they had travelled could go no further. With
them came typhus, typhoid, cholera, scarlet fever,
diphtheria, scurvy, malaria, and all kinds of skin diseases. No one really knows how many died; the
doctors were with the army, and no records were kept.
At every station on the long trans-Siberian railroad
carts were filled with the dead, who were thrown out
of the freight cars, and it was only in the early days
that there was time to make crosses and set them up
to mark the graves.

After an eight-day journey by train we left the
trans-Siberian railroad and struck south across the
rolling steppe toward the Caspian Sea. Our goal was
a little country hospital which had been closed for
several years. Our Quaker unit had promised to open
the hospital and to carry on the medical work of the
district. Probably no other thirty-bed ward ever saw
such a turnover of major operations and acute internal
diseases as began then. The line-up for our out-patient

department began each day long before sunrise. The village was fifty miles from the railroad and reached only by horse or camel transportation, yet it numbered eight thousand inhabitants and was the medical centre for sixty thousand people. All other hospitals in that district had been closed when the Russian doctors were called to the front.

The buildings were one-story log huts with walls a foot thick, and because there was no coal nor firewood in that treeless steppe region we had to heat the hospital and our dwelling-house with fuel bricks made from manure and straw. All the hospital laundry work was done by hand, operations were performed by the light of kerosene lamps, often dangerously tilted in the unexperienced hands of the husband, wife, father or mother who had brought the patient in. The most primitive sanitary rules were continuously broken by our neighbours. Because the village well had once been blessed by the priest, it could contain no harmful germs, even though all the barnyards of the street drained into it. When nursing babies cried they were given fresh cucumber or watermelon rinds to suck. Holy-church icons were kissed first by a diseased man to cure his disease, and then by a healthy child to keep it well. But when our methods actually effected cures the gratitude of the peasants was very touching.

I remember one Tartar patriarch from whose blind eyes our doctor removed two cataracts. When the bandages were taken off and the old man found that by a seeming miracle he could see again, he knelt and kissed the surgeon's feet, murmuring, "You are more powerful than Allah; for he smote me with blindness, and you gave me back my sight." We took no fees in money, but gifts of all sorts were brought to us, eggs and mushrooms, and fat geese and sometimes the beautiful linen scarfs embroidered in red and blue and black which the Russian peasants use for towels.

But those busy, routine days passed, and the rumour spread that civil war was drawing near our home. One rainy midnight, when there were only four women of us in the house, we were wakened by the tramp of boots on the porch and the sharp barking of our dog. Hastily jumping up, we found a dozen Bolshevik soldiers at each door of the house, the leader (a youngster of nineteen years) demanding admission to search for foreign spies whom we were said to be harbouring. It was at a time when the English and American forces were fighting the Red army at Archangel, and it was really strange that we had not been taken into custody earlier. As the soldiers entered the living-room our dog, who in spite of precept and example had refused to become a pacifist, snapped at one of the men's heels and was promptly quieted with a bullet through his throat. This shot, however, was the only unpleasant use of force. When we disclaimed the knowledge of spies or the possession of firearms the captain apologized for frightening us, and told off his men to search the house quickly but not to disturb any of our possessions. A quarter of an hour later the episode was over and the soldiers were marching off through the rain empty-handed, though all the neighbourhood knew that our trunks held several thousand rubles of good money.

Finally, one summer evening, we began to hear what we thought was thunder, but the Austrian prisoner who worked as orderly for us looked grave and told us that it was artillery—old-fashioned guns, he said, but quite effective in so far as our house was concerned. There was soon no question even in our minds as to the identity of the rockets which whizzed above us, ending in little puffs of smoke. Then the bridge connecting us with the nearest town was dynamited, and we had no more information about events except the distant view of civilians fleeing in all directions. Happily, we were about in the centre of hostilities, and as it seemed safer where we were than at any corner of the horizon we stayed on, literally beneath a three-days' bombardment, most of which passed high above our heads. The last day we spent huddled in the ice cellar while the Czechs chased the Bolsheviks through our gardens, with considerable damage to our potatoes and beans. In due time peace and order again emerged, and we could continue our refugee relief work.

Three years later that very area was the centre of the far more destructive force of famine. Fields which I left in 1918 shoulder high with yellow wheat, I saw in September, 1921, cracked and blistered from months of scorching drought. Less rain had fallen that year, it is said, than falls on the Sahara Desert. Dead horses and cows cluttered the roads, gaunt men and women with frightened eyes showed us the thin and dirty pancakes they had lived upon for the past two months, pancakes made of powdered grass-roots baked with the gelatine of dead horses' hoofs. In some places even these resources were exhausted and the people, to ease their hunger, were eating lumps of greasy clay. Hunting health was impossible in those days in Russia. All that one could do was to fight off death by bringing from America wheat and corn and flour and condensed milk to the starving millions of the Volga Valley.

Recently, however, the search for health has grown more successful. Since 1923 the Federal Department of Health in Russia, not having war and famine and pestilence to deal with, has undertaken extensive infant welfare work and has carried on anti-tuberculosis and anti-malarial and anti-venereal campaigns. With the advantages of a centrally directed and unified health system for the whole country it has, within the past ten years, reduced the infant death rate from twenty-seven per hundred to seventeen per hundred, it has doubled the numbers of doctors in the country, it has given every soldier a course in village sanitation and has turned hundreds of the old palaces into sanatoria.

In every city there are day nurseries where the babies of working mothers are cared for free of charge and where the mother is given lessons in the proper care of her child. Contrary to what I find is a very prevalent American idea, the Russian health authorities insist on the mothers caring for their own babies in their own homes. Through the provision of the state insurance funds each working mother is given a complete vacation of two months before and two months after the birth of the baby, receiving her full salary during this time.

On the outskirts of the larger cities one finds former country villas turned into forest schools—by which they mean boarding schools—for undernourished public school children, for whom the school doctors have ordered special open-air life and better food than they could obtain at home. They come in groups of twenty-five to thirty to these country boarding schools for three or four months' stay at a time.

All adults who are workers (and in this term are included mental as well as manual workers, such as clerks, school teachers, and lawyers) receive free of charge whatever medical treatment they may need. Even operations, hospital and sanatorium care are included in the free service. In other words, Russia has adopted a system of public medical work based on the same principles as the American public school system, counting that the provision of health as well as education is one of the duties owed by a state to all of its citizens equally.

The Quakers have helped at various points in the development of the new health work in Russia. You have read how we built a hospital in one remote town where, until our coming, the people had known nothing of medical service. To another village which already possessed a hospital we added a children's department, and installed in it a modern plumbing system and provided modern surgical equipment. In the fall of 1928, on the one hundredth anniversary of the birth of the world-famous author, Tolstoy, the Russian government planned to open a new hospital in the village of Yasnaya Poliana, which was his home, and in this hospital two Quaker workers were to act as nurses.

For over a year I worked in the Infant Welfare Institute in Moscow, part of the time teaching a group of sixty girls who had come from all over Russia to learn the proper care of babies. There were among them Esquimaux from Archangel, and there were also Tartars and Mongolians in the group. All these later went back to their homes on the fringes of civilization to teach the native mothers how to keep their children well. Some of the girls could barely read, but what they lacked in preparation they made up in zeal for their work. One, with tears in her eyes, came to me begging me to tell her in conversation about the lesson in the book, because she said that a book still frightened her and before a printed page her mind went blank; yet anything she was shown and told, she could remember perfectly.

A modern type of nursing service, especially good visiting nursing, is badly needed everywhere in Russia. The harsh living conditions and the precepts of the old religion have tended to destroy all reasonable attention to the care of the body in health or in illness. There are still not nearly enough doctors to handle the enormous medical needs of the rural population, but good nurses would double the effectiveness of those doctors now there.

Quaker adventuring nowadays has lost some of the outward excitement and romance of war and famine days; but in the attempt to understand the needs of another group of people, perhaps of a group that is often misunderstood, whether in this country or in some foreign country, there is still a challenge to those young people who are too thoughtful to be stampeded into the grooves of popular life.

XIV

WHITE BANDITS IN RED RUSSIA

The anonymous author of "White Bandits in Red Russia" served under the Quakers both in Poland and in Russia. His desire to be an obscure worker for the cause nearest his heart will not let him tell, even under the shelter of his anonymity, of his most stirring adventures, those which touched the deepest emotions of his heart. He does not want to make a show either of himself or of those whom he counts as friends. He was willing to write only such a story as many another might have written.

AT five o'clock one Sunday morning in May, 1922, Quaker headquarters at Sorochinskoye, in the province of Samara, Russia, was astir. This was nothing unusual. The work of supervising the distribution of food to 150,000 starving people in two hundred villages required long hours of work from the half-dozen Quaker men and women who had come from as widely separated places as Philadelphia and San Francisco because they had heard the call of the Russian people for food during the great famine of 1921–1922.

But this day was a holiday. The Quakers were going on a picnic. There was something of the nature of truancy in what they were about to do. The chief of police of the district had told them that they must not go anywhere without obtaining a permit from him.

123

Not that he would not give them a permit to do anything under all circumstances, for the Quakers, to whose coming in the latter part of 1921 most of the people owed their lives, were permitted to go anywhere; but there were bandits in the country, and the chief of police was responsible for the safety of his American visitors.

Also, he loved formality, and to be seen giving the Quakers permission to come and go increased his prestige in the eyes of the peasants. Consulting him, however, on this particular morning meant waking him up, and a long walk to his office. Then there would be papers and more papers, signatures and counter signatures, and a big red seal, the wax for which could never be found in a search short of an hour long. The Quakers were in a hurry. The best solution was to slip away at five in the morning, unannounced. They only hoped that their Ford would not stall as they passed the chief's house on the way out of the village.

This trip was to be a picnic, indeed, but work was to be accomplished also. The village of Mikailovka lay fifty miles to the southeast. Reports that half its population had died during the past winter had been frequently brought to the Quakers. They had sent food, but had never visited the village to see what actual conditions were. On this Sunday, the first day free from routine duties after the spring floods had subsided, and the first day the roads were fairly passable, the Quakers were going to make the long-postponed visit.

There were five people in the party—a professor
of economics from a Quaker college in the Middle
West, and his wife; a biologist from California, and
his wife; and last, but important, a farmer from
Pennsylvania.

When all was in readiness, when the picnic lunch
had been prepared, and Henry Ford well stocked with
Baku gasoline—Russian-made gasoline—the professor
of economics, who could always be depended upon to
think of details, reminded us of one thing that was
lacking.

" I think we had better have the flag on the radiator," he said, as he reached beneath the front seat
and pulled out a square red patch of cloth, and fixed
it to a short stick that was attached to the top of the
radiator. This flag indicated that the Friends were on
government business—feeding the people.

Henry Ford coughed violently on the Baku gasoline,
and back-fired a couple of times, but finally settled
down to a noisy sputter, and the party started off down
the long village street toward the distant, rolling, barren steppes. The villagers craned their necks through
the windows of the widely separated low mud and log
huts that lined the wide street, and half-dressed little
children scampered out to get a better look. But the
aspect of the sputtering, speed-make vehicle was
altogether too terrifying, and they retreated to the
houses.

As the crow flies, the distance to Mikailovka was
fifty miles. Unfortunately the Russian peasant does
not steer his cart as the crow flies, so the route was

fully a third longer. The roads were unspeakably bad. They lay through several villages. In each one the entire population turned out to see the strange American horseless " telega," and its, to them, even stranger American passengers. Information as to the route was easily available. Every peasant had voluminous information to give. The directions, which agreed in most particulars, were the ones followed by the Quakers in choosing the trail to Mikailovka.

By three in the afternoon the village was in sight. It was a large village of about three hundred houses, all facing on one long street. As they approached the village, the Quakers were dumb with surprise. In place of the outpouring of villagers from every house that had greeted them in other villages, here not a soul was to be seen. The houses were all closed. The shutters covered the windows. There was dead silence in the streets. Not a dog barked, not a child cried. The Quakers pulled up in front of the Dom Sovieta (headquarters of the village soviet), which was also the schoolhouse, a long, low building with a large porch in front. Its shutters were all closed.

The Quakers alighted from the car.

" What does this mean? " asked the biologist. " This surely is a village of dead people. The reports were evidently not exaggerated."

They were startled with a sharp command, " *Rooki na Verkh!* " shouted from the direction of the schoolhouse. In an instant the shutters and doors were pushed open, and a crowd of men appeared, some dressed as soldiers of the Red army, some as peasants, each holding a rifle or revolver levelled at the automobile and its passengers.

One did not need to know Russian to know that the command meant " Hands up! " The Quakers obeyed instantly.

" Search them," was the next command. This time the speaker was visible. He was a tall, black-haired, powerfully built man in uniform, who was evidently in command of the party. Three soldiers stepped out and proceeded to search the Quakers and their car. All papers were found and removed.

The commander then stepped forward.

" Who are you? " he demanded, in Russian, " and what do you want? "

The economics professor had by this time regained his composure, and, keeping his hands aloft, replied quietly, " We are the Quakers. We came to find out the condition of your village. We had heard that many had died of starvation, and we thought you might need more food."

" You have papers, of course," said the commander.

" Your soldiers have them now, our passports, and our identification papers from the Soviet government."

The commander turned and looked over the papers very carefully, after first telling the Quakers they might lower their arms. He conferred at length with some of the soldiers, and then, giving an order to the soldiers to ground their rifles, he came forward, his hands extended, and his tone full of apologies.

" *Tovarischi Amerikantsi*," he began. " Comrades, Americans, we have much to apologize to you for. We

have made a big mistake. You are not the ones we
were expecting."

" Whom were you expecting in such fashion? " in-
quired the farmer.

" Bandits, comrade, bandits. It is all the fault of
the bandits. What poor Russia has suffered! How
grateful we are to you who came to help us—and to
think how we have received you! How can we ever
tell you how sorry we are? We have made such a
mistake."

" What bandits? " asked the economics professor.

" Didn't you know, comrade, that there are bandits
in these parts? Didn't they tell you up in Sorochinskoye? There are bands of robbers, mostly remnants
of the White armies. They swoop down on a village
and take the best horses and cattle, and shoot whoever
resists them, and are gone before soldiers can arrive.
But we thought we had caught them in a trap this time.
A week ago we received notice by telegraph in Buzuluk
that a troop of bandits was terrorizing several villages
in this district. I came here with a few soldiers. We
received news yesterday that the Tartar village of
Yarkumshut, fifteen *versts* to the north, had been attacked by a band of about fifty bandits. Several of
the inhabitants had been killed. We expected that
Mikailovka would be attacked next, and so we got
ready for them in the manner which you have seen.
We saw you coming in your machine when you were
three *versts* away, and so we had time to order every-
one inside. We thought you were the bandits, who
had stolen a machine somewhere. As you came down

the village street I was on the point of ordering my men to open fire, but delayed because I did not want to make a mistake."

Villagers were crowding in from all sides. Every one wanted to talk and apologize and make amends for the mistake that might have been made. As soon as possible, the Quakers began the business for which they had come. A meeting of the village soviet was called. Reports were heard as to the conditions in the village. It was found that rumours of the great death rate in this village during the past winter, from starvation and disease, had not been exaggerated. Over half the villagers had died.

The Quakers promised more food, and then departed, and arrived back in Sorochinskoye very late that night.

About three weeks later, the economics professor met the tall, black-haired captain in the streets of Sorochinskoye. The captain told him a very simple, straightforward tale.

"Do you know, *Tovarisch Amerikanets,* what happened after you left our village of Mikailovka on your visit three weeks ago? Well, about two hours after you left, when we were all off our guard, the bandits did come, about fifty of them, all mounted. They swept through the village like a tempest, shooting at everything in sight. We finally succeeded in driving them off, but not until they had killed ten of our men. We accounted for fifteen of theirs. Comrade American, can you ever forgive us for mistaking you for bandits? And we might have fired on you, too. How can we ever be grateful enough to you for coming to help us? "

The Quaker for a moment was thankful that he and his party had escaped the bandits. Then he thought how the Quakers had failed to interest the great mass of the people of the world in the way of good will, the way which was saving lives here, both of bandits and of those who might have lost their lives at the hands of bandits. Governments must be taught the spirit of adventurous good will. His own government, in America, he felt, was taking the wrong path. Its agent, the American Relief Administration, forbade any woman to go to Russia as a famine relief worker under its direction. Yet women were doing deeds out here no man could have done, and they were as safe as in America.

XV

DOUKHOBOR PILGRIMS TO AMERICA

HOWARD W. ELKINTON, *who comes of an old Quaker family, is a Philadelphia manufacturer, with plants scattered all over the United States. Like half of the Quaker men giving this series of talks, he is over six feet high and broad-shouldered. He served in relief work in France under the Quakers, so he speaks from experience in describing hardships. His is the third generation of his family which has been interested in the Doukhobors and has helped them.*

THE smoke line soon grew into a steamship, its decks crowded with twenty thousand and seventy-three men, women, boys and girls. They were Russians, clothed in their highly-coloured native costumes, with handkerchiefs on their heads and wearing decorated blouses—the Doukhobors, or Spirit Wrestlers, from Russia. The day was bright and cold and clear, January 20, 1899. The harbour was Halifax. This was the largest single company of immigrants which ever crossed the Atlantic to an American port at one time, a ship-load of religious refugees emigrating to North America for religious freedom, probably the last immigrant group of this size that the world will see for a long time to come.

Persecution of the Doukhobors in Russia goes back many generations. Homes were invaded by the Tsar's secret agents. Husbands were torn from their wives, girls from mothers, and fathers from sons, and carted away in exile to the cold wastes of Siberia. Ten years before the American colonies broke the British yoke with the Declaration of Independence, two Doukhobor girls were whipped with rods and stripped of their possessions and sent into Siberia because they insisted God could be worshipped in other ways than as prescribed by the Russian Orthodox Church.

In 1892 an English Quaker, Joseph James Neave, living in Australia, felt in his heart that he must visit this persecuted people in Russia. A check unexpectedly came from England large enough to cover all of the expenses of such a long and arduous journey. He took boat to England at once. The English Quakers gave him credentials. A printer of Gloucester, in the west of England, by name John Bellows, heard the message in his heart, " If thou wast to be called to go with Joseph J. Neave to Russia, wouldst thou be willing to obey? " He obeyed. They went together to St. Petersburg, now called Leningrad. Here they obtained, after difficulty, the necessary permission from the Tsar's government to visit the unhappy Doukhobors, who at that time lived in the mountains of the Caucasus between the Black and Caspian Seas, whither they had been driven because they would not serve as soldiers in the armies of the Tsar.

I can never forget how, when I was last in Saskatchewan, Canada, the tears rolled down an old man's face as he stood in the circle of his fellows and told of the hardships of life in the Caucasus. He described how the Doukhobors assembled together on the 28th day of

June, in 1896, around a great fire, on which they heaped all the guns and arms which they had. He told how they destroyed these weapons designed to hurt others, and how the Cossacks rode down upon them. Rising up in their stirrups, they lashed to the right and to the left, with their horse-whips, blows that fell upon men, women and children. And as the cruelty rained upon their heads, the victims sang their songs and prayed to God that their enemies be forgiven for this wrong.

They were driven by two and threes back into wild Georgian villages. Families were scattered; they had to endure all kinds of abuse and suffering. The hope of the Tsar's government was to stamp out this people who refused to kill their fellow-men. The old man, with the tears rolling down his cheeks, told of these terrible things that burned so deeply into his memory as a youth. Those interested in further details will find them in a book written by my father, Joseph Elkinton, in 1903, called *The Doukhobors*. It is in many public libraries. Most of these libraries also have a book by Alymer Maude, on the Doukhobors.

When news of this persecution of 1896 reached England immediately a committee of English Quakers, aided by Count Tolstoy, of Russia, urged the Tsar to let this people go. They raised money for a wholesale emigration. Fortunately, the Russian Dowager Empress had passed through the Caucasus in March, 1898, at which time the Doukhobors pleaded for her permission to emigrate out of Russia. The permission was granted by the Tsar himself. But picture the English

Quakers sitting in committee in London when they received a cabled message, stating that three thousand five hundred of the Doukhobors had fled for their lives under renewed persecutions, without waiting for advice, permission or money. The English Quakers hastened to arrange for the first place of refuge. The British government permitted the people, driven like cattle, to collect on the island of Cyprus as a place of temporary refuge. A few weeks later the Canadian government invited the Doukhobors to the empty western prairie provinces of North America.

There was one provision in the Canadian law that made Canada a particularly attractive place for the Doukhobors. The Dominion militia act, in Section 21, states: " Every person bearing a certificate from the Society of Quakers, the Mennonites or Dunkards, and every inhabitant of Canada of any religious denomination otherwise subject to military duties, who from doctrines of his religion is averse to bearing arms and refuses military service, shall be exempt from such service when balloted in time of peace or war, upon such conditions and upon such regulations as the governor in council from time to time may prescribe."

People willing to suffer but unwilling to kill other people are a very great embarrassment to every government in time of war. It is needless to say that the Doukhobors in Canada became very unpopular between 1914 and 1918, but, to its credit, the Canadian government kept its word with them, and, as far as I know, with all other Canadian conscientious objectors. Canada is a land of religious freedom.

It was a bitter struggle, settling in the wilderness of the northwest. Trees had to be uprooted, ground had to be cleared, the soil had to be ploughed, seed had to be sown, houses had to be built and materials had to be got, or these people would have starved to death under the cruel winter that came down upon them. It was a bitter experience, but they worked hard. Perhaps some of you have seen pictures of Doukhobor women drawing the plough. Be not misled; the women drew the plough because the men were working on the railroad in order to earn money absolutely necessary for the purchase of goods. The Doukhobors hewed down the trees and used the trunks to make log cabins, which they covered with earth, laying out the villages as the villages are laid out in Russia—houses on a straight line, facing a wide central village road. They at first lived as they had in Russia, as communists. The village became the commune, so that each man, woman and child worked for the village and from it received his clothing and tools and food.

American Friends, or Quakers, were able to gather barrels of clothing, bales of wool and car-loads of spinning-wheels together with a train-load of food, which they sent to these homesteaders on new land. As years went on, the Canadian government insisted that their land should be held individually, or by a corporation. Some moved out on their own initiative, and individually purchased farms, on which they have been able to build, through tireless industry, well-painted modern houses and ample barns. Others refused to live out of the commune, and moved to British Columbia. Others agreed to live in a commune under the curious title of Christians of the Universal Brotherhood, Limited.

Today about five thousand five hundred of a total of fifteen thousand Doukhobors in Canada live in the commune. We think of communism as something new and connected with the Bolshevik government in Russia, but communism is a very old way of living in Russia. Thousands of peasant villages have been maintained for centuries on what most observers would call the communist basis. The Canadian government insists that the stock shares of the commune must have a limited liability. The Doukhobors, instead of distributing the stock to individual members, hold it in trust, with a board of directors, twelve of whom are elected each year by popular vote. There is one director for each of twelve settlements. Altogether the Community Corporation at present holds property worth approximately seven million dollars, two-thirds of which has already been paid for in cash. It is hard for us in the long-settled east to think of capital in terms of toil and work, uprooted trees, clearings, killing frosts and all of the disasters that surround pioneer developments. The Doukhobors have submitted to and worked through such handicaps. If you should visit their settlements in Saskatchewan, you would find well-cared-for farms, and industrious and simple-hearted people, known for their kind treatment of animals and their honest dealings with men.

If you should visit their communities in British Columbia, where they cut down the bristling spruce forest you would find lovely orchards, a modern jam factory, and an efficiently equipped saw-mill on the delta formed by the turbulent waters of the Kootenay and Columbia Rivers.

The picture of their religious meeting which I attended in 1924 is always a fresh memory. Early in the morning the Doukhobors began to arrive slowly, driving their wagons along the sandy shore of Devil's Lake. For the most part they were dressed in the old costumes, the men in plain clothes of the farmer, the women with their finely embroidered peasant handkerchiefs over their heads, beautifully banded skirts and aprons bordered with brilliant red and blue and green stripes.

The meeting was held in a grove of poplar saplings, with a loaf of bread and a dish of salt on a bare table to symbolize hospitality. On one side of the circle the men stood, and on the other side the women stood, as Russians always stand through religious services. The men would chant their song cadences, pitched in a curious plaintive minor key. The women would answer, joining in with the rhythm of the song. One's heart was filled with the pathos and emotion stirred by the songs that had been created under the persecution of the Tsar.

Russians enjoying speaking as well as music, the meeting lasted without interruption for three hours. Then long streaming linen cloths were stretched through the grove; on these food was piled, and the company, divided roughly by families, ate the mid-day meal. Many of the Doukhobors are still vegetarians,

basing their habit on a religious scruple that it is wrong
to kill animals for food. As a consequence, they have
developed many excellent characteristic dishes, such as
the Doukhobor " borstch," a delicious vegetable soup;
" kawas," a palatable cucumber soup which, when
rightly made, contains floating pieces of ice; waffles of
their own recipe and pies of great variety. They drink
water and milk and no intoxicating beverages. They
are on the side of prohibition—which has been argued
recently back and forth in the Canadian provinces.

Nobody pretends that all the Doukhobors are saints,
any more than that all Irishmen are saints—and my
great-grandmother was Irish! You probably have
seen somewhere, if you have ever heard of the Doukhobors, the story of the fanatical pilgrimage to meet
Jesus that a few of them took in 1902 across the prairie
toward Winnipeg, or you may have seen exaggerated
stories of burned schoolhouses. Every nation has its
few cranks; but the Doukhobors have served Canada
well and are a great company of honest, hard-working,
sincere people.

The Society of Friends, commonly called Quakers,
is still adventuring. Quakers are interested in these
people, whom they helped to escape from the old Russia, for whom they got boats to carry them over the sea,
and to whom they gladly sent what goods and money
they could collect, at the beginning of this century.
They are interested in them because they cling to the
belief that all war is contrary to the teachings and
example of Jesus Christ, and they share many of their
other attitudes.

XVI

JAPANESE BANZAIS FOR AMERICANS

Thomas Elsa Jones, the president of Fisk University, saw service under the Quakers in Siberia during the Great War. Later he was a professor in a Japanese university. While in Japan he saw the great earthquake and used his Siberian experience to organize the Japanese Quakers into an effective unit for relief of the earthquake sufferers. Later he returned to America, believing that here was the crux of the so-called race problem; and here he found what he regards as his greatest adventure, flinging his energies into one of the serious disputes which seemed to grow out of racial discriminations. He tells of the earthquake disaster and what he learned from it.

TWO-THIRDS of Tokyo had just burned up. The remainder of the city was a mass of twisted pillars and fallen roofs. A pall of smoke slowly drifted towards the Pacific. A stream of humanity, like a never-ending river, poured into this field of devastation on the main highway into the city. Half-clothed, smoke-begrimed, hollow-eyed refugees trudged their way to the country on the other side. Japan was mortally wounded. War fortunes had begun to collapse two years before with the failure of the Seventy-Fourth Bank, of Yokohama. Now they were hurled into a holocaust of destruction. In five hours one-eighth of the total wealth of the nation had vanished.

While buildings were still falling, Japanese Quakers fifty miles up country loaded a Ford car with rice and threaded their way through crowded highways to desperate refugees in Tokyo. Forty thousand homeless men, women and children were encamped in nearby parks without shelter or sanitary conveniences. The Japanese Quakers, with little resources but abundant faith, organized bands of young women to bring milk to babies and of young men to dispose of filth. Scarcely had they started when the wireless stations in Osaka picked up messages from the Quakers in America, saying that thousands of dollars and abundant building materials were on the way to Japan. A Quaker professor of economics in the Tokyo Commercial University, who had lost everything in the earthquake but the clothes on his back, organized a group of Japanese people to help children find their lost parents. The head of the Young Friends Association, the Young Quakers, assembled a group of young men to help dispose of the dead.

All this was accomplished within twenty-four hours of the earthquake. Within the next few weeks a model village, a social settlement, and milk stations were established.

While the Quakers were busy during these first days, the Japanese were shocked to see a fleet of American battleships steam into the harbour. Full of fear, they waited for the inevitable conquest of their helpless nation by America. And then it came—it was a conquest of good will! A new thing had happened. America had repudiated the opportunity for military

conquest, and now offered friendship and help. War-
ships had been turned into rescue ships, loaded with
food, building materials and money. Fear in Japanese
hearts changed into adoration. " *Banzais*," hurrahs,
for America went up from tens of thousands of throats.
Tear-stained faces beamed gratitude upon any for-
eigner thought to be an American. The Japanese felt
that they were a part of the family of nations which
had shortly before been formed at Versailles. This
thought changed anguish at loss into joy at friendship.
It was great to be an American in Japan in those days.

Then something happened. The Anti-League-of-
Nations advocates, the America-for-Americans enthusi-
asts and White-Supremacy doctrinaires joined forces.
They made plans to shut out immigrants, to segregate
the Jews, to put the Negroes " in their place " and to
make America safe for the upper caste of white property holders. Nine months after America had played
the rôle of angel of mercy in Tokyo, Japanese immigrants were excluded by law. America had repudiated
the gentlemen's agreement. Thrown out of the family
of nations by this elder sister who had so recently pro-
fessed love, Japan felt jilted, humiliated and disgraced.

" *Shitsurei desuga, konnichi chu genkan ni matasete
kudasaimasenka?* " " It is very impolite, but, if you
don't mind, won't you let me stay in your front hallway
today? " said a polite Japanese policeman to Mrs.
Jones on the day the exclusion law went into effect.
He explained that while they did not really expect
trouble, in order to make doubly certain, the government had decided to protect every American until the

excited opposition to this unfortunate law had died down. He pointed out that the Japanese could not understand how the America of the war period, how America, the sponsor of the Washington Conference, and the heroine of the earthquake relief, could be the same country which had now humiliated Japan.

America appears somewhat like a big, prosperous, sympathetic, generous but crude adolescent. Blunders such as this are not meant in a bad spirit, we all know, but often when it is too late the discovery is made that real injury has been done. I felt sure that the root of our unfortunate treatment of Japan was based upon a philosophy of racial difference erroneously assumed to exist between white and coloured people. I was keenly desirous of helping my country right the wrong done the great and sensitive nation of Japan. I went to see what I could do at Fisk University, located at Nashville, Tennessee. I wished to know the facts about race. I was sure that the so-called facts which had appeared in books about the Negro were as distorted as those which had appeared in other books about Japan. I wished to know for myself and at first hand.

I have not regretted this venture. New vistas of American greatness opened before me almost every day. The possibilities for moral and social leadership which this great nation possesses in view of its wealth and position are fairly staggering. We can and must find a solution for the race question. If we do, we have gone a long way in solving our other international and interracial problems. We attempted to justify our exclusion policy on the ground that we wished to put our house in order. We said we wanted to give equal opportunities to all American citizens. We have failed to keep this pledge. We have been pouring millions of money into white education and but a few thousands into Negroes education. We have segregated the Jew, the Italian and the Pole. Terrorism, lynching and race riots have been common during the last ten years. Yet we have and are making progress. State aid for Negro education has been increasing. Lynchings have steadily decreased. Many people are giving Negroes more privileges, although a few persons are giving them fewer.

We must study the facts. The test of a nation's greatness is the way it treats minorities within its body politic, and the way it treats weaker republics in other parts of the world. If America is to maintain the friendship of Japan she must treat her with respect. If she is to strengthen the best qualities of the Japanese people—and they have a patience, loyalty, astuteness and skill which America may well covet—we must show confidence in them and give them a chance.

To get the best results out of our contacts with the Negro tenth of our population, we must give them adequate opportunities to obtain sufficient education to win a livelihood, to acquire property. We must help them to heighten their self-respect and increase their diligence. We must provide them with schools. We must give them opportunities to develop their capacities to the full. The old master-servant status of feudal Japan had to be replaced by group honour, group ethics and group loyalty in the present social order. So the Negro servant will render full service, keep his appointments, and be loyal, in proportion as his Negro leaders are educated to convince him that he should keep the job he has. That he must work for earnings with which to improve the status of all in his group.

When we help the Japanese nation abroad and when we help the Negro group at home " to be somebody " we will raise their standards of living, and cause their wants to increase. They will conserve their money as capital, and their purchasing power will be enlarged. Frequent exchange of ideas of the leaders of all races will teach us that the interest of the best Japanese, the best Negroes, and the best white people are identical. When this is made clear, officials will be chosen as public servants not because of any pet theory of race, but because they stand for an honest and clean administration for all people. Churches will not be snobbish and draw a Pharisaical robe about themselves, but will hail as brothers all who stand for righteousness and fair play.

Let us wipe out the blot against our good name with Japan as soon as possible. No " yellow peril " is confronting us, and no Oriental horde is ready to pounce upon us. Japanese wish to be our friends. They will not intrude where they are unwelcome. They will treat us with honour if we respect them.

And let us delay no longer to fill up the gap between Negro and white education. We have nothing to lose and everything to gain. The Negro is interested in other problems. He wants the rights to food, safety, home and an education. And in so far as these are granted to him will it be easy to grant them to all races and nations. In so far as this is done will the foundation for a permanent peace be established. The earthquake relief showed America at her best; let the challenge of the race question keep that best continually to the fore.

XVII

IN THE PENNSYLVANIA COAL FIELDS

SOPHIA H. DULLES *served in reconstruction work in France after the war, under the Quakers, and later in child feeding in Germany. In telling of the coal fields of Pennsylvania she speaks with authority. She speaks as one who has seen the destruction, suffering and misery caused by war.*

O NE doesn't have to go abroad to find Quaker adventures. Right here at home today the American Friends Service Committee is in the midst of as big and as adventurous an undertaking as ever took its workers to France or Russia or Germany. The committee is answering the call for relief of the innocent victims of the bitter industrial struggle now going on between the soft coal operators and miners in the eastern United States. The committee is neutral. The Quakers look upon this relief work as an emergency measure *only*. In tiding the young generation over the present crisis, they hope to get knowledge of the coal industry that will be useful in reaching a solution of the mine problems. The work is being done without propaganda for either side.

It was on April first, 1927, that the organized soft coal miners of Pennsylvania and Ohio were called out on strike; some had already been locked out. A few papers carry strike news, but it is only by going out into the coal fields and mining camps, stricken as if with paralysis through these long months without work, that one can picture the tragedy that lurks behind the news.

We read that on the first of April, 1927, the Jacksonville agreement between operators and men ran out; that the operators refused to renew the wage scale, saying that it was too high for profits, that the men refused to accept a reduction. The other day I asked a striker out in Indiana County why he didn't quit the union, and get a job in any mine at any wage, to earn something for his very large and hungry family. His answer sized up the wage situation briefly and vividly. He said, " I don't throw over the union and go back to work at the rate they offer—the 1917 wage scale—because I'd rather starve sitting down in the sun, than starve at work in the dark underground! "

So operators and strikers, sixty thousand strikers, lie clenched in a death-grip in these great rich northeastern coal fields. We, the consumers, are getting all the coal we need from the non-union south and west. We cannot see what is happening up among the hills of Pennsylvania and Ohio. We soon forget that there is a strike, and rest secure that our famous American standard of living will see that no one is *too* hungry, and that it will certainly provide medical care for the sick and dying.

In January, 1928, the American Friends Service Committee decided that it was time to get the unvarnished facts of the situation. Alarming rumours were in the air, rumours of suffering and of death from want.

So they asked two women to go out and see and hear for ourselves, and to make a report. I haven't time to tell you all the story, but if I can give you some faint idea of what has happened in one town only—one of the larger ones—you can fill it out, for after all it is just repeated, on various scales, in camp after camp, valley after valley.

Until six or seven years ago, this bituminous coal town, like the others, was comparatively thriving and happy. The war boom had brought prosperity. Shops, banks, even moving picture theatres, sprang up. It boasted the Americanization of its numerous foreign-born inhabitants. It taught them, with pride, to live according to what we call our American standard. The mines were working full time—the Jacksonville scale brought in an average income of twelve hundred dollars, though this is scarcely half the family budget prescribed by the United States Department of Labour even then. There is no industry in that part of the state except mining, but the mines were working, all right, and why look ahead? The accident rate was so high as to make it better to leave the future to itself, anyhow; why worry? So they didn't, until the tide turned—until business started to leave the valley. The non-union fields were beginning to catch the orders; work got slack here; the mines shut down in summer, or cut time to four, to three, to two days a week; the town's trade began to stagger under the strain.

Then came the wage cut—thirty-three and a third per cent at once. Miners, tradesmen, moving-picture theatres—these were trapped together up among those hills where they had invested their all—they were trapped in the net of an industrial crisis for which they were not responsible. What could the men do? They could strike. They could fight, as they say, " not with raised fists, but with folded arms! " And it looks as if they would go on fighting, as they believe, to save their union and their right to live.

My fellow-worker and I arrived in this town in central Pennsylvania, in the middle of January, 1928. The day was dark, a half-hearted snow was falling. Snow fell, in those high places, three days out of four through a winter that seemed endless. Two streets that make up the town skirt the flank of a long hill. The rows of rickety houses are of frame, unpainted or partly covered with the remains of sickly yellow, olive or brown paint, because on the more sheltered sides there is still some left to peel off. Built on the steep hillside, the houses rest on props in front. They look very light and unsubstantial. It almost seems as if they have just perched there to take breath and are about to fly away again in a minute.

Below, in the bottom of the valley, are mines, with shafts marked by their great black wheels that let down the cages. In every fork of the valley are mines; above, high up on the hill, are more mines—slopes, these are called, with openings not much larger than the doorway of a fair-sized dog kennel, with narrow-gauge tracks running out of them like long black tongues. The tracks run down across the town to the valley, where towering piles of rejected coal smoulder through the day and glow in red flaming patches in the night. They burn through spontaneous combustion—can't be put out, just go on burning until they are exhausted. They throw off suffocating sulphurous fumes. The heavy smoke rises slowly, as though some giant were continuously burning incense to the god of modern industry.

The heart of the town is where a steep road crosses the main street. On two of the four important corners stand the two banks, known as the red bank and the white bank. On the third corner is the general store; on the fourth, the hub of the whole district, stands the corner drug store.

There must be peculiar virtue in that corner, that bit of pavement, that view. Banks and shops are deserted, signs announcing extraordinary sales, and bankruptcy notices, stare from the windows; there is no traffic or movement in the street, but those four corners are never empty. Union chairmen and officers favour the drug store corner, the other three have their devotees and faithful stand-patters, too. There they stand tonight, every night, the strikers, unutterably pathetic, in groups and singly, silent, motionless men, muffled in shabby cast-off coats, gazing before them. In the winter, when the wind cut too sharply, a few stepped under doorways for shelter, but the rest stuck it out. We wonder if they are watching for that something that one feels must come soon, to break the spell, or curse, of inaction that lies on the town.

This town has normally a population of forty-five hundred and a union membership of ten or twelve hundred—a strong union centre. To these hundreds have been added other hundreds, refugees from the surrounding smaller camps, increasing the misery, families evicted from company houses in places where the union has not been able to put up barracks to lodge them.

At some nearby camps, long scrambling rows of union barracks line the hills. From the doorways the miners' wives look longingly across at the boarded-up windows of the company houses that they have occupied, and even contrived to love, for twenty and thirty years! If they lived in a company-owned house, they and their belongings are now crowded into one or two rooms in a flimsy, leaky barrack, or in part of some old house. If they lived in a rented house, the rent is mounting up as a debt, there being no money to pay it. If the family happened to own its house, they have already, months ago, gone the limit on mortgaging it. They have nothing with which to pay the interest or taxes. Any day may see them turned out, and that will be the end of their life's savings. And when the strike is settled, at last, and the mines open again, and the whistles blow and work begins—the blacklist is still to be gotten past. The more active men, the leaders, and, so often the older men, look forward to the blacklist as their Waterloo.

The chairman of the local union, a man of sixty, said: " It was the blacklist, after just such a strike as this, that drove my father out of England and over here. He went from mine to mine, and every time he was promised a job, it went to some one else. So we were starved out and came to America. I started work underground here at ten years old. I wonder if there is any place left to move on to? "

And what about the miner's wife? Well, she is having all the disadvantages of striking and of being overworked at the same time. Her family now is just as big as—sometimes bigger than—before the strike or lock-out, and every one is just as hungry. The union weekly relief allowance, when it comes, is seventy-five cents for each parent and twenty-five cents for each child, up to three dollars a week per family; so if you have more than six children, more than a dollar and a half's worth of children, you are out of luck! Bread, coffee and potatoes are a common diet.

It is always the children that the women ask us to help—even the shiftless women. One said to us: " We grown-ups can make out somehow, but it sure is terrible my kiddies missing all this school because we can't get 'em shoes! "

Food and clothing are both lacking. As a miner expressed it, " Lots of the little ones haven't on enough to cover a canary! " The small children depend for warmth on the family stove.

In one house we found three, too young for school, running about barefoot, as usual, and dressed much as the miner described. By the door stood a pair of enormous torn men's galoshes. Suddenly the boy of seven ran to the door, put his little skinny feet into the galoshes and shuffled out into the snow on some errand. Later the door opened, and in he shuffled, his silhouette in the doorway much like Charlie Chaplin, stopped again beside the door and solemnly stepped out of the galoshes, leaving them for the next member of the family who should want to go outdoors. We found schools where half the children lacked under-clothing.

One urgent plea for help came from a school principal who wanted us to give food first of all to the high school students. He said that the basketball team had lost every game this season, and when he had recently questioned the boys one by one, after an especially bad defeat, each had confessed that he was simply too hungry to be able to play. Not long ago the state nurse told me that she had just seen a note from one of the mothers asking that her children be sent home at the 10 o'clock recess, as she had not had a crumb of breakfast to give them; some one had promised to give her a little bread, and she hoped to have it by then.

One Polish family we chanced to find just when a neighbour, also a striker, had brought them the first food they had had for twenty-four hours. The only complaint they made to us was a remark of the mother that when she has been working for some time she gets " light in the head."

Perhaps the most tragic part of all is the plight of the sick. Doctors, like the shops, are stopping credit. Only a short time ago a striker in this town was sick with pneumonia, and, being penniless, no doctor would go to him. At the very end one doctor relented, but it was too late—the man was already dying. Babies are being born without a doctor's care. In the town of which we are talking, the local Red Cross has now arranged to meet this unbearable condition, in part, by providing a doctor for ordinary cases. This is the only such action which we have found in the five mining counties we have come to know, and cases of child-birth are not included even here. What is to become of the many expected babies, and what is to become of their mothers?

And this misery must be multiplied a thousand times. In valley after valley, in camp after camp are just the same dreary scenes and events. About one and a half million people, strikers and their families are caught in the net of this industrial catastrophe. Add to these the wretched strike-breakers who drag from camp to camp in search of a living wage and a decent life. For the strike-breakers are not flourishing and well fed. Behind all this looms always the incalculable power and violence of the coal and iron police, of deputy sheriffs and of state troopers, reinforced by injunctions that forbid anything, forbid picketing, forbid giving food to hungry children.

These things are happening here, not in post-war England, or in famine-stricken Russia, or in defeated Germany, but right here in the richest, proudest nation of the twentieth century, in our own booming, industrial, luxurious United States. After the war, when Europe was in want, we poured out money and workers to help to save her children. The American Friends Service Committee is giving food, milk and graham crackers, in the schools, to the most seriously under-nourished children of thirteen mining towns already. We have also given hundreds of pairs of new shoes and outfits of under-clothes, as well as quantities of used clothing, but the need is great.

Whatever the future holds for our mine workers, their children are bound to suffer from all this stupidity and bungling of us of the older generation. If the strike continues, hunger, want and disease will flourish. When it ends, the fathers will go back to work—if there is any work for them—at a wage scale lowered by about a third, and heavily burdened with new debts. Yes, we Americans helped to save the children abroad after the war and famines; the call for help, at home, today, for our own children, is just as real!

XVIII

WITH FAMINE AND SCOURGE IN SYRIA

ELEANOR W. TABER *is well qualified to speak from the Quaker point of view. She is clerk and presiding officer of the joint business monthly meetings of the Quaker congregations of New York and Brooklyn. She cannot mention the names of the people who played the most thrilling parts in the adventures she knows of, nor will she be able to tell details of most of these adventures until the actors have passed away, unless a new government arises which knows not the old hatreds. She has travelled extensively and knows the Near East as a traveller as well as a worker in an orphanage. She tells of a country of Druses, Syrians, Jews and Arabs under a French mandate.*

THE Quakers started schools in Syria nearly fifty years ago, when Syria was a part of Turkey, and when Ras el Metn was a long day's donkey ride from Beyrouth. Ras el Metn is a village of two hundred houses stretched out for two miles on the very crest of a narrow mountain range. It looks down over terraced hillsides to the blue Mediterranean in the distance. The walls of the stone houses are three feet thick, and many of the homes still have flat mud roofs on which the peasants dry their wheat and pine cones. The richer families live on the second floor, which is cooler in summer and less damp in winter, but the poorer families have to live on the ground floor.

156

In the early days Ras was very isolated. Once, when one of Daniel Oliver's children was sick, he sent to Brumana, on the next mountain, for a doctor. Dr. Manassah came on horseback to prescribe for the little sufferer. He left medicines and arranged that Mr. Oliver should light a bonfire that night to signal how the child was. This seemed an easy way to signal the news, for the two hilltop villages are within sight of each other, but the Quakers never dared use it again, for a rumour started that the Quakers lit the fire to burn babies. That was long ago; today all the country people know that the Quakers are their friends.

The Syrians of the Lebanon Mountains struggle to earn a scant living from the stony soil, they terrace the mountain side, plow the little patches of level ground with their cows and plant wheat, grapes, olives and mulberry trees, for silk worms are an important crop.

The World War brought untold suffering to the Syrians. After Turkey sided with Germany, she requisitioned for the army the wheat grown in all the larger valleys. This left only the wheat of the smaller valley, the Ba'kaa, to feed the civilian inhabitants, which meant that the price of bread would be high. Then, in 1915, came a plague of locusts. The locusts flew in clouds darkening the sun, and when they settled they covered the ground so that no one could take a step without crushing them, and one could hear the noise of their eating as they destroyed every blade of grass. There was no wheat left to make bread, no food for the women and children. In time of peace, wheat could be brought by ship from Australia, but during the war the ships of the world were too busy carrying munitions to take food to such a little country as Syria.

So the people went hungry, and as they grew weaker disease increased—typhus and typhoid and malignant malaria. Women and children wandered about from village to village begging bread, unconsciously spreading disease as they went. Often they fell dead on the road.

As the famine grew worse Daniel Oliver sent word to America of the suffering of the Syrians. America not having declared war on Turkey, we were able to send money to Mr. Oliver for relief work. He started a bread line so that the women and children of Ras el Metn and some of the neighbouring villages might have at least a little bread each day. Don't ask me where the wheat came from to make that bread! I suspect that every man who owned a mule too old or too lame to be used in the army, drove his mule by devious paths over the Lebanon and Anti-Lebanon Mountains to the Hauran, where grew the wheat intended for the Turkish army. And I am afraid that those lame mules carried back very heavy loads of the life-giving food.

Well, somehow, Mr. Oliver got his wheat, and day by day the number of women and children in the bread line grew. It was winter now, cold with the thin chill that comes at an altitude of three thousand feet, when the wind blows from snow-covered mountains. There was even snow on the streets of Ras el Metn.

One evening Daniel Oliver sat thinking of the children to whom he had given food that day, thinking of one tiny boy who wore only a single cotton garment. Mr. Oliver grew restless; he could not put the thought of that boy out of his mind. He got up and, taking his lantern, went out in the road to search for the boy. Soon he found the child, asleep in the snow, with no covering but a little cotton shirt. Mr. Oliver carried the boy home, warmed him and fed him, scrubbed him, and cut his hair. The next day he could not bear to turn the little fellow out, so he kept the boy. Soon there were other homeless boys to be taken in. Before he knew it, Daniel Oliver was running an orphanage.

It is of that orphanage I want to tell you. I lived there for five months in 1925. The war was over. Syria was settling down under the French mandate. The younger boys could hardly remember those evil days, but the older ones, youths of seventeen, eighteen and nineteen, remembered all too well. During school time they were too busy to think of the past, but in vacation, after a few days of holiday joy, we could see that they were brooding over their lonely condition. Mrs. Oliver often said that it was impossible to feed a boy who had been through the famine so as to make him grow fat.

I have been asked to tell you of adventures. To me the everyday life of the orphanage was one great adventure such as I would never have the courage to undertake. Imagine running a home for one hundred boys where every drop of water for washing had to be carried in old gasoline cans from half a block to a block, where all drinking water had to be brought from a spring a quarter of a mile away. Imagine cooking for a family of one hundred on one fair-sized kitchen range. In good weather the cook used to boil the beans on a small fire out of doors.

Today the boys have good dormitories built over the school-rooms, but until 1924 they had to sleep in the school-rooms at night, and by day roll up their beds and pile them against the walls. (In the Near East a " bed " is a quilt spread on the floor as a mattress, with another quilt used as a blanket.)

It requires courage to bring up such a large family of children thirty miles from a doctor and with no telephone communication. Of course, Mr. Oliver has become expert in administering castor oil and quinine. He pulls teeth and administers first aid generally. I rolled miles of bandages for him.

All the people of the village call on Daniel Oliver for medical advice. Often they would quarrel among themselves and shoot or stab each other. One such quarrel ended in Saleem receiving a bad knife wound in the arm. Mr. Oliver advised him to go to the hospital in Beyrouth for treatment, but Saleem was obstinate and refused to go. The wound became infected, and the man grew too weak to stand the journey to Beyrouth. A doctor was called, who said the arm must be amputated at once. The doctor could perform the operation, but needed some one to administer the anæsthetic. Daniel Oliver volunteered to help him. They cleaned up the little one-roomed stone hut as well as they could and moved the man near the single unglazed window. But when they began to operate all the neighbours came crowding round the window until the light was cut off, and they had to stop the operation to order the people away. Saleem got well.

This last winter Mr. Oliver had to be away from Ras el Metn for four months. He left Mrs. Oliver in charge and, to make it easy for her, arranged to have an English trained nurse stay at the orphanage and care for the children's health. Hardly had he left when a bad epidemic of dengue fever broke out in that part of Syria. Mrs. Oliver and all the teachers and most of the children came down with the sickness. The nurse had her hands full caring for so many patients,—and then she took the disease herself. Fortunately, she had trained one boy to help her in the dispensary, and that boy had to care for all the others.

I spoke of the boys' remaining at the orphanage until they were eighteen or nineteen. This may seem old to you, but remember they have all lost three and four years of schooling. It is Mr. Oliver's policy to keep all boys who are bright enough to profit by schooling until they graduate from the Syrian equivalent of high school. They are then qualified to become teachers in the primary schools of the country, or to take good positions in the business houses in Beyrouth. A few have gone on to the American University at Beyrouth, but that costs money, about three hundred dollars a year for board and tuition.

The boys are fine fellows with plenty of character. They speak and write three languages, their native Arabic, English and French. They are used to hard work, and are, oh, so eager for an education. Mr. Oliver has had to make a rule that no boy shall get up to study before 4:30 in the morning. In vacation time all school-books are locked up to prevent the boys trying to study ahead.

Some of the boys belong to the Greek Orthodox Church, some to the Roman Catholic, a few are Moslems, but probably most are Druses. (The Druse religion is one of the secret cults of Syria.) Ras el Metn is a Druse village, as you can easily tell by the white cloth the men wear wound around their red *tarbouches,* while the women wear white veils. The Druses live at one end of the village, the Greek Christians at the other end. Today there is comparative good feeling between the two sects, but even now a Druse seldom eats a meal in a Christian's house, or vice versa.

Many times, even within the past ten years, men have quarrelled over their respective religions and have started to shoot each other up, to prove which is the true religion. Mr. Oliver would rush out and try to make peace; he would persuade them to put up their guns and go to bed. The next day he would begin to pay formal calls on the chief men on each side, trying to get from them the true story of the affair and to persuade them to keep their hot-headed young men in order. Perhaps several days would be consumed in these calls before all the details of the peace could be arranged. Then, on two successive days, the leaders of the parties would hold feasts, at which both parties would solemnly seal the peace by eating together.

I had heard of these riots but did not think much about them until one evening, when we heard shouting and quarrelling under our windows. I caught a glimpse of Mr. Oliver's face as he rushed out to see what was the matter. He was white as a sheet, and his face told me how serious those previous fights had been.

While I was at Ras a fine old Danish gentleman came to visit us, Pastor ————. He is not a Quaker, but I must tell his story. He and his wife and niece lived half a day's automobile ride beyond Damascus, out in an oasis in the desert. While they were staying with us the Druse revolt of 1925 broke out. We on the coast were safe enough, but their consul in Beyrouth refused to allow them to go to their inland home. The roads were infested with brigands taking advantage of the upset political conditions to rob any auto that came along. And the oasis was a long way from any sort of governmental protection. Of course, his Bedouin neighbours knew and loved the pastor, but there would be constant danger from strolling bands.

The pastor was most anxious to get back to his people. At last he persuaded his consul to let him go. Early one morning they started in their touring car. I wish you could see the load that car carried. Besides the three of them there was a trunk, moving picture machine, innumerable suitcases, bags, water bottles, and eleven golf sticks. Both running-boards were entirely filled so that the passengers had to climb in over the doors. Well, the bandits spared them, and they reached home in safety.

Some months later the French army and the Druses had a skirmish near the pastor's home, after which the French manœuvered quickly to another position, leaving two wounded men behind them. The wounded men crawled to the house, begging aid. The pastor took them in and nursed them. The Druses heard of this and came to the pastor, demanding the soldiers. The pastor invited them into his parlour. There they stood, the frail old man against the wall, and, with their guns pointed at him, again demanded the Frenchmen. But the old pastor was not to be cowed. He replied that the Frenchmen had come to him asking hospitality, and he could not give them up. The Druses were silenced, for no Druse will violate the sacred right of hospitality; they left the brave old man to take care of his wounded men.

I could tell you many tales of that land of sunshine and high mountains. But I can only say, Go and see it for yourselves, go and enjoy its boundless hospitality. You will find the people jumping in one generation from the age of the camel to the age of the automobile. If you are a woman physician and want to reach out into the unusual, go and settle in one of the mountain villages. You will have many strange experiences while earning a good living, and you will alleviate untold suffering; for, while most of the women might describe their symptoms to a man doctor, few would allow him so much as to put his stethoscope on their chests.

As the Syrians say, " *Saadi in baruk.*" May your evening be peaceful.

XIX

RELIEF FOR SERBIA'S UNDERNOURISHED

SAMUEL ELY ELIOT *was born in Portland, Oregon, but had a varied education in the east and west, including three years as Rhodes scholar at Oxford, England. In addition to being director of settlements and other experience in social service work, he has had business experience. He and his wife spent a year in Serbia in relief work under the Quakers, and he looks back on that year as full of memorable experiences.*

M Y wife and I went with the American Friends Service Unit of a dozen workers to the heart of the Balkan Mountains in old Serbia in October of 1919. The different members of the group undertook a mixed job of medical, agricultural and relief work. We were among the relief workers.

We arrived at Salonika, in northern Greece, by the usual means of transportation—steamer to Patras, on the western coast of Greece, and railroad from there through Athens to the busy, semi-oriental port of Salonika.

Later we saw the soft, brown hills of Macedonia roll by. In the spring, I suppose, they would be green— where not too rocky. Then we saw the first green valleys of the south of old Serbia, where the whitewashed walls of the farm-houses gleam in the sunshine and the poplar trees grow along the streams, and the minarets of old Turkish churches in the villages point up at us like fingers from the ground.

A little toylike train makes interminable stops at the towns and big villages. At one station, the village brass band gathers, composed of a half-dozen tattered, gypsy musicians with battered horns and trumpets and a slack bass drum. They tune up their wild music, while the passengers, disembarking from the train, amuse themselves with their native dance, the *kolo*, until the train makes up its mind to start again.

We would see occasional water-oxen, those broad-horned cattle with humps on their shoulders, which always suggest the Orient. Indeed, Serbia, or Jugo-slavia as we now call it, is the first European nation with a flavour of the east. When you first arrive there you find yourself unconsciously beginning to think of Arabia, or China, or Japan.

There would be a great temptation to stop in the town of Leskovatz, a hundred and fifty miles north of Salonika, where our unit of workers first established itself for several weeks, while planning fields for our efforts. Here is the little meadow opposite the hospital compound where Mrs. Eliot and I sat at the foot of a hay-stack on a mellow October afternoon intending to wrestle with the Serbian phrase-book. But a kindly peasant who was tending cattle there approached in courteous fashion and, finding us to be speechless foreigners, proceeded to help us with the rudiments of his language. He squatted in the stubble field and gradually got over to us a vocabulary of elementary words which I shall never forget,—the terms for shoe, coat, hand, head, tree, grass, etc., etc. Never have I had a better teacher; he was patient, his voice was soft, his smile was friendliness itself.

Later Gospodja Panitchka, the characterful, humourful school teacher with the voice of a traffic cop, helped us further in our struggle with the Serbian language. Her lessons, however, were frequently converted into vivid and elaborate accounts of Serbia's suffering during the war. She spoke German, which we could understand. Gospodja—which means Madame or Mrs.—was herself beaten on her bared back by Bulgarian officials because of her stubborn refusal to comply with their orders as to what Serbian children should be taught. She introduced us to many leading families of the town.

We went with her to their *slavas*. Now, a slava is a celebration held by a Serbian family on the saint's day of the male head of the family. Every one with the name Michael celebrates Saint Michael's day, for example. Saints' days come pretty thick, and I read recently that by government action Serbia has cut out thirty of them in order to increase the efficiency of the nation, because on a popular slava day no one pretends to work. When a family celebrate their slava, there is open-house all day long. Relatives, friends and, theoretically, strangers, especially the poor, are welcome. The house has been marvellously garnished for the occasion. For weeks before the day, the women have been washing, scrubbing, baking and stewing.

The Serb's hospitality is perfect in its naturalness, its simplicity and sincerity. The humblest peasant or the most cultured city official, any and all of them, seem to have a native gentility in their intercourse with others. And the "eats" at a slava! Choice syrupy fruit preserves—quince, grape, strawberry or plum, and an infinite variety of mysteriously delicate and rich cakes in which you can taste pine nuts and spices. A special cake was made of swelled wheat grains, mixed with honey; pressed into a mould and turned out on a plate. And then tiny glasses of wines, including Serbia's national strong drink, corresponding to whiskey, called *rakia*, made from prunes. When the Turkish coffee comes, it is the polite signal for the guest to begin to get ready to depart and the Serbs have their merry jests over this point.

Leaving the north-and-south railroad at Leskovatz we strike west over a wide plain (wide, that is, for Serbia), on and on across the rolling foothills until, after thirty miles, the mountains become more rugged and forest-clad. Following the line of a military road, we see the sharp rocky summit of Tulari Mountain, which thrusts its head up higher than the rest of the ranges at a point directly opposite the tiny village where Mrs. Eliot and I spent the first five months of the year 1920.

I said "village;" but you might say, "Where is the village?" In the sparsely settled portions of the Balkan Mountains, a village, as likely as not, consists of a church, a town-house, a schoolhouse, a *kaphan* (that is, an inn), a gypsy blacksmith shop, and possibly half a dozen houses of officials or wealthier farmers living at the cross-roads. The main population is clustered in groups of a half-dozen or a dozen farms, each at a spot favourable for farming or grazing. Thus, at Tulari, there were seven or ten supplementary farming communities, each with its own name and identity, scattered about the ridges and valleys of an area forty or fifty square miles in extent. From the top of Tulari Mountain the Serbs loved to point out to us these irregular patch-quilt communities, speaking of each one with fond familiarity.

About five miles down that road is the first field big enough to warrant the name of meadow. I was back and forth over that road many times. There you will find five or six children tending sheep. They have deserted their games, similar to our mumbelty-peg or hockey, which they play with sticks and stones; or, if the day is cool, they have abandoned their little fire, which often they hunch around to keep warm. Or, perhaps they would be coming along the road home from school with a little pack of books on their backs, and in the spring they would surely be picking wild flowers from the road-banks.

I have never seen such wild flowers; and, except for the violets and wake-robins, they are all a little different from ours. Primroses grow riotously along these beautiful valleys. And the nightingales sing gloriously at night.

In the middle of the war the Bulgarians and Austrians had temporarily conquered Serbia. Her army and many of her people had fled, but the sturdy mountaineers formed guerilla bands and continued their resistance. These bands, knowing the mountains like a book, were able to support themselves with the provisions supplied by the women, children and old people who continued to run the farms. It was an easy matter for a small scout band to come up to an isolated farmhouse at night and carry back to their comrades in the mountains the food and other necessaries which had been secretly assembled for them. Bulgarian troops, endeavouring to cope with this type of warfare, suffered the fate that Braddock endured at the hands of American Indians.

Finally, the Bulgarians determined to destroy the sources of supply; namely, the farm-houses themselves, and they went through the country with torches, setting fire to the thatch of thousands of farm homes. In the early fall, four members of our unit, fine boys from Quaker colleges, had co-operated with the British Serbian Relief Fund in rebuilding many of these homes, in a district just to the north of Tulari. Sixty Bulgarian prisoners were assigned to them for this work, which had to cease when the snow began to fly.

These workers turned their hands to the rehabilitation of an agricultural school for boys, which was near Leskovatz, and which the Bulgarians had partially ruined by converting it into a stable for their cavalry. The medical members of our unit meanwhile discovered the need of health work over the border in Montenegro, and their efforts were focussed on establishing a hospital in that field. It fell to Mrs. Eliot's and my lot to enter this mountain district of Tulari by ourselves.

In this region we fed the undernourished children from the American Relief Administration supplies; and gave what rudimentary medical assistance we could. Consequently, we established our residence and headquarters in a building which had been the village townhouse. When we entered it, in the middle of a bitter January, it was nothing but an abandoned shack. It had been used as a camp and stable by the Bulgarians, and its mud walls were riddled with bullet holes. There was no window glass, no wooden flooring, no chimney. However, few Serbian houses in the mountains actually are provided with chimneys. Smoke from the fires simply finds its way out through the tiles or thatch of the roof. Scraping away a couple of inches of hard packed dry cow dung, we laid a tent down on the mud floor, set up our little gypsy-built sheet-iron stove and began housekeeping. Muslin covered the one window of the room. A bright peasant boy, Petko Vuksanovitch, helped us with wood and water. The spring was ten minutes' climb up the mountain. It was a wonderful life. The peasants swarmed around us with curiosity and friendly interest. Our equipment seemed meagre enough to us, but to them we looked like a whole department store.

The *predsednik* (mayor) of the town and the council of village elders waited on us to discourage us from continuing our residence in such an unprotected spot. "Albanians will attack you at night and kill you for your possessions," said they. We were only a few miles from a mountain border beyond which the Albanians had controlled things until one of the recent Balkan wars. Every able-bodied male carried a rifle around these mountain districts. Cattle raiding was common. We, of course, had no weapons of any character. Several times on moonlight nights when lying awake I had a few moments of sober reflection about how easy it would be for some bands of drunken marauders to make a target of our gleaming white house. But that was the nearest thing to fear at our home which I personally experienced.

When I recall that I left Mrs. Eliot for three or four days at a time during trips back to headquarters and that her sole protector was our thirteen-year-old Petko, it seems reckless now. But we trusted the people, and I suppose there is nothing under the sun that goes so far as that simple state of mind. There was one cause of fear, however, that we succumbed to entirely, and that was the Serbian watch-dog. He is fiercer probably than the fiercest wolf. Indeed, he is half wolf anyway. On the road once, I was backed against a high precipitous bank with two dogs attacking, one on each side. My stick was good for only one dog at a time. The breathless peasant who saved me gave the simple instructions, " Carry a stone! "

Our home was about two hundred feet from the schoolhouse, which made the feeding of the children a simple matter. The schoolmaster co-operated with us. We borrowed a great copper kettle and in it Mrs. Eliot cooked cocoa mixed with dried milk. Allowed to simmer for several hours, this mixture provided a delicious and very nutritious food. The homespun clothes of those forlorn children were in absolute shreds. Their cheeks were pasty yellow, almost grey with malnutrition. Their hair had that peculiar dry-straw look, which occurs in a child who is underfed. Their eyes were staring and lustreless. Yet these boys and girls tramped those muddy mountain trails from distances of five and seven miles for the few hours a day of unspeakably inadequate instruction which their teacher was able to give them.

Such a school! Only one or two windows with glass in them. Most of the winter all the children had colds and frequently expectorated in the school-room. The teacher sat on the table and never took off his military hat. Did he rule with the rod? When he was not lifting a child off the floor by the hair or an ear, it was his rod that he used freely. Military discipline? The first words that all Serbian children learn to write in their copy-books are, " Gladly goes the Serb into the soldiery "!

Every day at the same hour the long, long line of school children would form, gripping in one hand the little tin cans in which the dried milk had come and which now served as cocoa-cups. We learned to be thrifty in that faroff mountain spot. We do not need our kodak pictures of these children to remind us of the gratitude, expressed in face and eye rather than in words, which these children felt for this soul-satisfying nourishment.

There was sickness of every kind. When people were seriously ill we referred them to the British hospital outpost, fifteen miles below us towards civilization, but we suddenly found ourselves practicing medicine without a shred of a license when it came to skin diseases, indigestion, and minor injuries. We ran a lively clinic.

The peasants tried to repay us with eggs, or a hen, with honey, or the hind leg of a rabbit, or again with bowls of a native cream cheese called *kimac*. This is one of the most delicious dishes I have ever tasted; in fact, I got fat on it. But not until after I had been made sick by their bread, which has a little bit too much roughage and mill-stone grit in it for an American stomach. Mrs. Eliot also caught influenza while attending a serious case in a snowstorm. She lay the third day in a fever and while the church bell tolled its liquid note through the mountain valley, for the death of another victim, she only said, languidly: "How sweet it sounds!" The presence and the thought of death were constant companions in Serbia. But I have never regretted this close-up acquaintance with it. Whether or not it is a touch of Oriental fatalism in him, the Serb is so familiar with death that he does not seem to fear it.

However, we both recovered, and enjoyed the most glorious springtime I ever hope to experience. If you want to see people scintillate with joy, stay right here in the heart of the Balkans and watch the peasants come to life after a hard winter. The sunshine, the new leaves, the bleating lambs, the fragrant soil and, probably above all, those gorgeous blossoming fruit trees and wild flowers, all mean more to these people than we can dream of. They put a nosegay in their cloth hats or head kerchief, and dance and sing, and enjoy life in a way I sometimes think we mechanicalized western barbarians have forgotten or—maybe never did know about!

XX

AMONG AMERICAN INDIANS

LAWRENCE E. LINDLEY *was trained as a scientist and made soil examinations for the United States Department of Agriculture. When the United States put the draft law in operation he applied for permission to serve in the Quaker Relief Unit in France. After being detained in a military camp for a year he was finally permitted to enter that unit. He remained in France in this work for about eight months after the armistice. Upon his return to America he and his wife went to live among the Indians in Oklahoma. Five years later the Indian Rights Association invited him to go east as one of its secretaries, and now he makes his home in Philadelphia.*

THE faint roll of tom-tom and drum assured us that our Indian friends on the back seat of our Ford were dependable pilots through the loose sandy roads of the country of the Big Jim Band of Shawnee Indians. A few more turns on the winding drive through the scrub-oak woods brought us to a large cleared space. In the centre of this space was a pile of corn bread and squirrel meat. Around the edge, seated on logs, were Big Jim Indian women dressed in red and blue calico dresses with long full skirts, each with a wide ruffle at the bottom. Some wore braided ribbon turbans with streamers of red and yellow and purple ribbons hanging down to their ankles. On each cheekbone was a brilliant spot of scarlet paint. Off to one side, under an arbour of leafy branches supported by poles, were four or five men wearing short, loose trousers and loose jackets or long-tailed shirts. They were beating the drums and tom-toms we had heard and chanting the song for the dance.

In a large circle about the pile of corn bread and squirrel meat the men were moving forward and bowing to the rhythm of the drums and accompanying chant. Their faces were painted in contrasting patches of yellow and green or streaks of black and white or zig-zags of red. Some wore blankets with red, yellow and green figures about their shoulders, others long-tailed shirts. Most were bare up to the knees, and some almost to the hips; all wore moccasins. The solemn dignity of the dance was punctuated every half-minute by spontaneous shouts and wild leaps of individual dancers.

This lasted fifteen minutes, then the men sat down around the edge of the dance ground and the women started their dance, a gentle even movement forward accompanied by a low chant set to the rhythm of the drums. After their dance of about fifteen minutes, the two groups danced at the same time for fifteen or twenty minutes, men and women in separate circles. So the ceremony went on from sunrise to sunset. They were dancing the Bread Dance held every spring as a prayer for good crops addressed to their female deity called grandmother. No devout Big Jim Indian plants his seed until after this dance. In the autumn they dance it again as thanks for the crops of the season.

The Big Jim Band of the Shawnee Indians selected these sand-hills with their scrub-oak trees and unproductive soil when the tribe was moved to Oklahoma because they thought the white man would never want to come here. They thought they could hunt wild turkey, squirrels and other game, that they could live their own lives, unmolested forever. But white people moved in and the turkeys and game are gone. So now the Indians need helpful friends with sympathetic understanding hearts. The old men spurn the white man and his ways, but the Indians turn to any true and patient friend. The children of the tribe are in school; the younger men are taking up improved methods of farming; the windowless, one- and two-room log cabins with dirt floors are giving way to more comfortable homes. The Big Jim Indians, forced by the coming of the white man to give up their old life so dear to them, are utilizing some of the advantages of the white man's civilization.

Nearly every one knows of the Osage Indians because of their great wealth derived from oil. There are only about two thousand of them. Some of these Osages often spend a few days at Black Dog Camp. Black Dog Camp is a group of houses in a grove, ordinary dwellings or large single-room buildings with screened openings on all sides and used for lounging or for dining rooms. In the centre of the camp is a small eight-sided building about eighteen feet in diameter with a roof running up to a point and topped with a cross. We are invited to the closing half-hour of the peyote meeting in this small building. We hear the monotone of the drum and the dried gourd rattle. We enter the smoky atmosphere and see a number of drowsy men lying about. Over at the opposite side of the room, cross-legged on the floor, sits the leader of the meeting, his face streaked with red paint, wearing a bonnet of eagle feathers, yellow buckskin moccasins and leggins decorated with red, green and white bead-work, with a blanket of red, green, yellow and white stripes and interlaced hooked designs, drawn about his shoulders.

In front of him is a dish of *peyote,* the dried top of a small Mexican cactus, looking something like halves of dried peaches. Resting against the dish is a crucifix. In his right hand he holds a gourd-rattle and in his left a fan of eagle feathers. At his left is the drummer. One man gives constant attention to a small fire burn-ing in the centre of the room. Our friend motions us to a seat on some Indian blankets. One or two men, remaining seated, give four- or five-minute talks in their native tongue, there is a pause and then I am invited to speak. Arising, I recall briefly William Penn's fair dealing and friendship for the Indians in the past and assure them that the Quakers today want to continue in this spirit of fair dealing with them; that it is our desire to be true friends to them and to share with them our experience of the heavenly Father, and that together we shall seek that fuller and better way of life taught and lived by Jesus.

Because of the narcotic effects of *peyote* it has been freely used by some of the Indians as a medicine. Cases are known in which it is believed death was caused by such use of it. Generally the effect is slow, resulting in indifference, physical weakness, loss of will-power and weakened resistance when attacked by disease. It is only within thirty years that it has been widely used by Indians in the United States. The usual mode of taking it is to chew the buttons and swallow them or to grind them into a powder and make a brew for drinking. It produces hallucinations, often with pleasant colourful effects. This and its stimulating properties seem to be the reasons for its hold upon the Indians. They say they see beautiful visions of Jesus and are enabled to live better lives, but *peyote* has been used in the ceremonies of pagan forms of worship among the Indians in Mexico from time immemorial,—long before the coming of the Spaniards and the Gospel of the Cross. The Osage children often remain at home and attend the Sunday School held at the Quaker Mission instead of going to the *peyote* meetings.

In central Oklahoma are the homes of a group of Kickapoo Indians. Here in our faithful Ford we bounce over rough and bumpy roads or wind in and out among the trees along either side of the driveway and finally come upon a group of grass wickiups that look like elongated bowls turned upside down. We go to one of these winter wickiup homes and, pulling back the curtain door slightly, call out our greeting, " Ho-o," and ask if we may come in. The nineteen-year-old daughter makes us welcome. We seat ourselves on the pile of grass rugs that line the edge of the room. In the centre of the wickiup a small fire is burning and over it is hung a kettle of soup. A hole in the top of the wickiup serves as chimney. In one corner is a small table and a few shelves for the kitchen equipment. The girl is making dough for biscuits. She rolls it out, places the biscuits in the frying-pan-like oven which has three legs, rakes a few coals out of the fire to put under and above the frying-pan and sits down to talk with us. In one corner of the room is a pile of grey blankets and comforters; in another a couple of trunks, indicating clearly the inroads made by the white man's civilization.

The girls in this Indian family bear the name of Frye, taken from the well-known New England Quaker family by that name who have done so much for the Indians. One of these Indian girls, Myra E. Frye, was raised by two Quaker women missionaries who lived among the Kickapoos, and now she lives in Wichita, Kansas, and takes an active part in the Quaker Meeting there.

Along with the simplicity of this home you also see the problem of sanitation with its dirt floor and small confined living space. Added to these is the ignorance of the Indians concerning diseases and how diseases spread from one individual to another. It is hard for the boys and girls to come to such homes after they have been away to government boarding school where they have become used to modern conveniences.

Close to the foothills of the Ozark Mountains in northeastern Oklahoma is Wyandotte, a village of one hundred and fifty people, where we spent the last two of the five years we worked in Oklahoma. Here we dealt with about two thousand Indians, full-bloods and mixed-bloods, some wealthy, some middle class, and many very poor. Several miles out in heavily wooded country is a clearing and a two-room log house, with a neat yard, which a flower-bed brightens. Greeted warmly by the Indian family, we enter the larger room, which is both living-room and bed-room with one tiny glassed window. Mud fills the cracks in the log walls. Newspapers cover the walls. For furniture there is a dresser, a sewing-machine and three beds, for in this room sleep the four children and the parents. The floor is bare. The smaller room at the back is kitchen and dining-room, with a shabby little stove supported by stones to make it higher. The household has little clothing, almost no food,—and there is sickness. We have brought them clothing, food and medicine and friendship. Crop failures, sickness and white man's trickery have ravaged this little home. But we still find courage there. From homes like this came most of the hundred and sixty children in the Wyandotte government school where we held religious meetings, twice a week. At these meetings twenty minutes' instruction was given in Old Testament stories, the life and teachings of Jesus, stories of brotherhood or missionary activities. The remainder of the hour was filled with singing of hymns.

The Indians are today as ready to co-operate with the white man as they were in the days of William Penn. I have attended burial services for members of the Osage tribe. The words of one young Osage man, spoken beside the open grave, will never leave me.

"For many centuries," he said, "our fathers roamed over this great country leading a happy and care-free life. The whole land was ours. Then your fathers came and settled among us. Now we live, white man and Indian, side by side. We must be to each other friends and brothers."

XXI

IN WAR-TORN IRELAND

WILLIAM W. PRICE *is a Philadelphia architect who served in relief work under the Quakers in France during the war. After he had returned to his professional work, following the close of the war, he was sent to Ireland with five other Quakers as part of a group to report upon the need for relief work there. The members of this group were all trained observers who had had wartime experience in France, so Mr. Price's story is a plain unvarnished tale of what life means in a country torn by civil war. His story covers only the experiences of a forerunner sent to observe, and does not deal with the relief work which followed.*

SOME seven years ago, when the quarrel between England and Ireland was at its height, I had been reading in our papers about the Black and Tans, about reprisals and the burning of houses and creameries, and had wondered vaguely, what a Black and Tan was. Accordingly, when in January of that year I was asked to go to Ireland as part of an investigating commission, I accepted with alacrity. There were eight of us, six of us being Quakers, and we travelled over Ireland in pairs, covering the whole of the island pretty well.

I remember our introduction to curfew. That word may bring up in your minds a picture of a girl swinging on the clapper of a bell, or of a whistle or bell at dark, to send children to bed. But curfew in Ireland in 1921 was much more serious than that. No whistle was blown, no bell was rung, but the first thing one did on entering any new town, was to ascertain the hour of curfew—be it six in the afternoon or ten at night. It was said, and with reason, that if you were caught out on the streets after curfew, you would be shot, with no questions asked—until afterwards, when it might be too late.

We had come into Cork in the afternoon, and after supper we went out walking. The streets were full of people, Irish girls walking with unarmed British soldiers (no enmity here, apparently), and all sorts and conditions of others. Curfew being at nine o'clock, a few minutes before that hour we returned to the door of our hotel, remaining there to watch. At five minutes to nine there were apparently as many people walking up and down as ever. At three minutes before the hour, no apparent diminution in the numbers of pedestrians. At nine o'clock not a soul was to be seen in any direction, up or down the streets. And on the hour the curfew—trucks, loaded with their " Black and Tans " and soldiers, rumbled down the streets, each man's rifle barrel resting on the high sides of the truck and each man's finger on the trigger.

We were interested in seeing how we would be received in Ireland. We soon found that the common people, the non-combatants, working in fields or walking in the village streets, would first stare at our car, with its great placard, " American Relief Committee," in the windshield, then smile, and perhaps shout, " God bless you. Hope you'll do us some good." The British authorities were uniformly courteous and cordial. I remember one evening when they went even further in their solicitude. We had come into Limerick in the afternoon and had gone to the commanding major, in his headquarters, surrounded by barbed wire and pacing sentries, to obtain an extension to our special permits. He was most affable but regretted that the necessary blanks were at the police barracks. However, he promised to send them to our hotel in the evening.

The papers arrived safely, and I tried to call up our major, to thank him, but was unable to get him, so went off to bed. Curfew was at ten o'clock, and at that hour all the electric lights went out. Wilbur, my partner on that trip, was forced to come up to bed with a candle. He had just set it down, and was taking off his coat, when the first of the curfew trucks rumbled down the street outside. The second truck stopped, and Wilbur, at the window, announced that a big military searchlight was mounted behind it. This was at once evident, for the great light was focussed on the front of the hotel, sweeping slowly down until it struck our windows and its glare lit the room beyond the need of candles or electric lights. In fact, we could have done with less light, for the searchlight's beam stayed with us. And at this moment a hard knocking at the hotel door came to our ears. Next we heard voices and then heavy steps coming up the stairs, and towards our door. Someone called, " Is Mr. Price there? " And as soon as I could catch my breath I answered, " Yes! " Then the door opened, and a captain of police, in his black uniform, followed by two British soldiers, came into the room. The soldiers posted themselves at each side of the door, with drawn revolvers, and the officer came over to the bed where I was lying, and looked down at me.

"Are you Mr. Price?" he asked again, and again I gasped, faintly, "Yes."

"Well, Mr. Price, we were going through the city to see that every one was in bed and so we stopped in to see if you were in bed, and comfortable, and to ask whether you had received that permit?"

I gasped my relief and thanks and called Wilbur out from under the other bed, and the officer's eyes twinkled a little as he wished us good-night and went off with his armed guards and his searchlight.

So, you see, the British authorities even put us to bed at night.

Another time, as we were just leaving a small town down in what was called the war zone, we were stopped by a huge tree, freshly cut, lying directly across the road. In the car were the Irish chauffeur, my friend Wilbur and a photographer we had picked up in London. This fellow now jumped out and ran toward the tree to get a photograph of it. It was his first sight of the real "war-measures" we had heard of, and he was thrilled. It was only after he had returned to the car that he wondered what would have happened had there been Sinn Feiners, members of the Irish Republican army, hidden behind the obstruction. His question was easily answered, for we were all absolutely sure that he would have been shot without parley. We had to make a long detour around the tree and had just come back into the main road again when our car stopped suddenly. We saw a man coming towards us from the hill at the side of the road, with a drawn revolver in his hand. He leaned in at the window and his eyes were those of a fanatic.

"You're Americans, are you?" he questioned, and we started to produce our passports and papers.

"That's all right. We can trust Americans," he said, and then, ascertaining that the chauffeur was Irish, turned to young Boville, the photographer.

"You're American, too," he asked, and Boville answered, casually.

"Why, no. I'm English."

"English!" he cried, and I have never heard such hate concentrated in one word. With that, he pressed his revolver against Boville's chest and started to haul him out of the car.

We interfered at this point, explaining that Boville was working for our committee and that we would be responsible for him. The Irishman did not want to let him go, but at last consented, and then, turning, waved along the road, calling: "Get down, get down." We leaned out to see to whom he was talking, for we had seen no one.

There, as far as we could see, the hills along both sides of the road were lined with armed men—staring down at us. At his call, they got down behind trees and bushes and stones until not one was visible; and so we drove on through the ambush, not knowing through how many others, unseen, we had come.

And now just a word about the situation of the non-combatants—those caught between the millstones of the war. Suppose that we are an Irish family back in 1921, sitting by the fire in a stone-walled, thatched-roofed cottage. There is a knock at the door, and half a dozen young men, armed and masked, enter. They say to the father of the family, " There is to be an attack on the British troops down here on the road about a quarter of a mile away tonight. If you move out of your house to give the alarm, we will come back and kill you and burn your house down." They go out, and the family sit trembling, not daring to step outside. Perhaps later in the evening they hear the shots of the battle down on the road. But they don't dare to move. Perhaps even the next day they are afraid to stir.

At the evening of the third day there comes another rap at the door, and a jaunty young British officer enters. He says something like this: " Mrs. ———, you were here the other night when there was an attack on our troops. You must have known about the preparations for the ambush, for it was only a quarter of a mile away. Yet you chose to sit here safe in your house, instead of coming to warn us of the attack. To punish you for that, we are going to burn your house down. You have one hour to get out."

In the actual case of this kind which we met, the family's first knowledge of the ambush (it had been five miles away) was the arrival of trucks full of British soldiers, armed with bombs and gasoline cans, and the handing in at their door of a typewritten notice, giving them an hour to leave. They showed us that notice when next day we found them, huddled in one end of their bombed, burned dwelling, dazed—wondering what they had done to deserve their fate.

It was to help these innocent bystanders in the fight, the policemen's widows, the people, on both sides who had lost their all, that we went over. And I am happy to say that, upon the committee's recommendations, money was sent over from America and distributed to the neediest sufferers. One of the things in our experience most interesting to a Quaker was the fact that the eight of us, unarmed, were able to travel all over a war-torn country, trusted by both sides, with no worse experiences than those related. Two of us saw an English soldier shot down in reprisal in the streets of Cork, one of us nearly had a bayonet run through him because he had his hands in his pockets and so might have been concealing a revolver; we were all searched time and time again, but we all returned safe and sound. Some weeks after our return to America, Arthur Griffith and Michael Collins went over to London, sat down with Mr. Lloyd George in Downing Street, and arranged that South Ireland was to be a Free State—an arrangement that bade fair to solve the Irish problem at last.

XXII

FOR GOOD WILL IN NICARAGUA

Carolena M. Wood manages her own ancestral farm in Westchester County, New York, raising seed corn with a reputation of almost fifty years behind it. She was the first American woman to enter Germany after the war, and later was head of the Quaker child feeding in the occupied zone. Afterwards she visited Mexico, as one of a group, to investigate social and economic conditions there. Last year, with two other Quakers and a member of the Fellowship of Reconciliation, she was sent by the American Friends Service Committee in co-operation with the Fellowship of Reconciliation to report on conditions in Nicaragua.

FOR over three weeks I formed part of the American occupation of Nicaragua. I am not a marine, however, but a woman come from a line of Quaker ancestors who long ago enlisted in the great upward struggle of finding ways for fair dealing and understanding and friendship between people, races and nations so that hatred and fighting might be done away.

I landed in Nicaragua early in December—not from a battleship but from an Indian canoe hollowed out of one of the huge trees that form part of the tropical jungle which almost covers Nicaragua. I had not planned my arrival in such a way. That morning we had left San Salvador near six o'clock in an ordinary gasoline launch which each Friday crosses the Gulf of

Fonseca to Nicaragua. At noon we had been delayed
in picking up the mail bags that had come down from
Honduras, their one weekly mail, so that we were late
as we turned near dusk out of the swell that found its
way in from the Pacific Ocean and pushed at full
speed up a broad river, hoping to be able to cross the
bar and get to Tampisque on that high tide.

As we turned into the last stretch of narrow, winding water, leading through the dense mangrove trees,
we had only a few moments to spare. The engine was
doing its best as we dodged this fallen tree or that
heavy bush, when we stuck with full force upon a
sunken log. Americans and Nicaraguans were thrown
into a heap, in which there was no trace of imperialism,
and by the time we were on our feet again, the obvious
duty of all was to bail for our lives. The water was
rising fast in the boat, and in a moment the engine
was short-circuited, and stopped. Visions of alligators,
lurking among the roots of the trees, filled our minds.
There was apparently no human being for miles about
us, when suddenly an Indian dugout canoe appeared,
five men in it!

As they came alongside, the order was given,
" *Mujeres primera*," " Women first," and we five
women were soon safe with our new-found friends.
Just as it tells us in the story books, there was also
one man who chose to be numbered with the women,
in a place of safety.

As we paddled across the bar to the little settlement
on dry land, I found that our rescuers were members
of the newly-formed Nicaraguan National Guard, and

that their leader was a captain of the United States Marines. My first sight of the American occupation of Nicaragua! The guard had noticed that our launch was late, and thought they might catch us landing munitions for the rebel general, Sandino, but they landed us instead, of which we were very glad. In a few moments another canoe had been sent to rescue the men and the baggage.

We must not stop to enjoy the wonder of my all-night ride in an ox-cart drawn by four splendid oxen through the tropical jungle lit by a glorious full moon as we skirted the face of a high cone-shaped volcano. By six-thirty in the morning, we had reached the town of Chinendega, and were ready to enjoy the first meal we had had in twenty-five hours. I find that if one has enough excitement one does not get hungry so often.

At Chinendega we realized the reason for the marines being in Nicaragua—the appalling sight of a town destroyed by guns and fire hardly a year ago, when two political parties had fought there and destroyed their own beautiful city for the hatred and rivalry of politics. Civil war involving the whole country had been very close to them in the months that were past when Mr. Coolidge sent down Mr. Stimson as well as a thousand of our marines to find a way of peace.

What Mr. Stimson did was to make both parties give us their arms. We paid every man ten dollars for his gun. The money to pay them we took out of their own national treasury. Now our marines are the only people who are armed in Nicaragua except one general with his men. When Mr. Stimson made his offer to both the armies, General Sandino, who was with the Liberals, said he could not trust the United States to have the only power in Nicaragua. He said that even though the politicians of both the parties agreed to it, Nicaragua was his country, and a foreign nation should not take charge of everything; so he and his men went away into the mountains with their guns, leaving the ten dollars behind them.

They agreed to die as a protest against foreign occupation. They are still in the mountains. Mr. Stimson said that if they would not lay down their arms, the dignity and the prestige of the United States demanded that they should be forcibly disarmed. Thus it has resulted that as we ate breakfast each morning in Managua, we would see the aeroplanes of the United States flying off to watch among those volcanic mountains, to see if they could catch sight of Sandino or his men, and—later—then hurrying back to send huge bombing planes to drop their bombs to their cruel work below.

As the simple Nicaraguan peasants carry in to market their loads of coffee on their gentle ponies, they are passed by great motors from the United States toiling up the well-nigh impassable rocky roads loaded with guns and munitions to kill Nicaraguans on their own soil. They do not understand.

Sandino was our reason for going to Nicaragua. We had felt sure that if some quiet friendly people should have a talk with him, it would be possible to find a way of co-operation instead of war.

We had letters of introduction to his friends. They promised to guide us to him through the hard mountain riding for three or four days. They said the only danger was that the marines might shoot them. We Americans would be safe, but not they; so we went to the colonel of the marines to get a pass for them. Then we discovered some of the difficulties of an occupation. The colonel agreed to let the Nicaraguans go, but he said to us, " You cannot go."

We explained that we had not come to ask for permission for ourselves—that we were going anyhow. But he was adamant. He said Sandino was a bandit; that he would be only too happy to hold us as hostages, that then it would be the colonel's duty to drive through to rescue us, at any cost to the life of the marines, and that when he got there, he would find only our four heads, on four poles.

We explained that though that was an interesting picture, it was not necessarily correct. That if we were held as hostages, neither we nor our families wished that we should be rescued by marines; that we wished to try this method of saving our country from a serious danger of spoiling the affection of many Latin-Americans just at the time of the Pan-American Conference at Havana; that we thought it only fair that he should let some pacifists give their lives for their country as well as the marines. We explained that Quakers had always made a specialty of bandits, that they did not enjoy killing us, that our heads never had been put on poles, and we believed they never would as long as we kept a friendly spirit. Quakers are not afraid of bandits.   Bandits are not so different from ourselves.   Some great thought takes possession of their lives, and drives them to do things we do not understand.

All was of no avail.   He let us go to the mountains to talk with Sandino's wife.   We also had good talks with his father and brothers.   *They* said he was not a bandit, but a man with an intense love of his country. We met many fine and thoughtful Nicaraguans who said, " Are you really helping us by sending your marines? "   The President of Costa Rica said, " Can you not send school teachers instead? "

We did not see Sandino, but at least many Nicaraguans realized that there were friendly people in the United States, and this has comforted them.   We have just received a letter from General Sandino's father in which he says, " I repeat the expressions of my gratitude for your praiseworthy deed in leaving the tranquillity of your country for the sole purpose of seeking to bring harmony to these peoples, and to avoid the useless shedding of blood resulting from these struggles.   It would have greatly pleased me to have had you reach, with my son Augusto, an honourable and worthy peace.   However, we do not lose hope that events will shape themselves, with the aid of Providence, in a way that will show us the path leading to having back with us our son, and also regaining the peace of my country.   ' May the God of Nations watch over us.' "

As we came from our little adventures for friendship in Nicaragua, we felt sure that our present occupation of Nicaragua is incomplete. Even the fine fellows in our marine corps cannot adequately represent the great heart of America. Even our bankers, with their helpful loans, cannot accomplish it. There are opportunities for endless adventures in friendship if only our government could learn how to use them. The colonel of marines said, "I will not hold up military operations for five minutes for you to try such a hopeless experiment." But there surely are new ways of doing things.

There is a great unexplored country of good will that lies before us. We must have courage to go forward into that country and explore it. It is a country full of untried possibilities for the uplifting of mankind.

XXIII

HAITI AND THE AMERICAN OCCUPATION

PAUL H. DOUGLAS, *a professor in the School of Business and Administration of the University of Chicago, and a well-known sociologist, went to Haiti to represent the Quakers on a mission of investigation sent by citizens of the United States. His report upon the " occupation " represents the personal observations and the thought-out conclusions of a careful student of sociology.*

SEVENTY miles to the east of Cuba lies the island of Haiti, one of the first islands of the Caribbean to be discovered by Columbus, to which he gave the name of Hispaniola, and where he was buried. On the mountain slopes can be seen the huts of the black Haitian peasants, who raise on their small and crudely-tilled plots coffee for export. Although vestiges of voodoo worship still prevail in some parts, the Negroes are in the main peaceable and inoffensive, but their ignorance, poverty and isolation have in the past made them the victims of tyrants. In the span of a few years, the Spaniards killed off all of the original Indians, and then began to import Negro slaves from Africa to man the plantations. The French acquired control of the western part of the island and there built up, on the basis of slave labour, a rich sugar colony. The French Revolution aroused

197

dreams of economic freedom among the blacks and political freedom among the mulattoes, and after a complicated series of wars, the Negroes, led first by Toussaint L'Ouverture and later by Dessalines and Christophe (whose life has recently been told by John Vandercook in his book, *Black Majesty*), and aided by yellow fever, succeeded, in 1806, in driving out the French and exterminating virtually all of the white population. They were the first and indeed the only section of the Negro race to free themselves from slavery at the point of the sword. This fact, together with the cruelties which they had suffered at the hands of the whites during the period of slavery and later of civil war, combined to give them a great national pride and a strong dislike of the whites.

For one hundred and nine years this Negro nation continued to be independent, at first in the form of an empire with Dessalines and, later in the north, Christophe as emperors. Then it became a nominal republic, although in reality the republican form was merely a disguise for a series of military dictatorships. Few presidents indeed even witnessed the inauguration of their successors, since they generally succeeded in escaping on a steamer before the troops of the revolutionary army could occupy the capital of Port au Prince. From 1911 to 1915, the changes in government were especially kaleidoscopic, there being no less than seven presidents in these four years. Yet in all of these revolutions no foreign lives were ever lost, nor was any foreign property damaged. The Haitians knew that if this were to occur the aggrieved country would be likely to intervene, and hence refrained from any act of hostility. Haitian revolutions were therefore for domestic consumption only.

American influences also helped to hasten the disintegration of the Haitian government during 1914 and 1915. We tried to get Haiti to turn over her finances to our supervision, although she was not in default on her foreign loans, and we also tried to have her set up a constabulary under our control. Haiti refused to do this, and the National Bank of Haiti, which was the official depository of the government and in which American firms had a one-fifth interest, refused to turn over any of the current funds to the government but insisted instead on impounding the revenues for a year. This shutting off of the funds seriously crippled the government and made revolutions easier.

Finally, in July, 1915, the murder of one hundred and sixty-five political prisoners by a subordinate of President Guillaume Sam led the populace of Port au Prince to rise and assassinate Sam. American marines were landed from the American cruiser Washington with the proviso that they stay only long enough to restore order. That was nearly thirteen years ago, but American marines are still maintained in Haiti, and we control the government of that country. We succeeded in having a president elected who was favourable to our policy and, by dint of seizing Haitian custom houses and by the threat of force, pushed through, in November, 1915, a treaty which gave us control over finances, the constabulary, public works and sanitation. Whether by accident or design, however, justice and education were not included, and the schools and courts have until recently been under Haitian control.

The treaty was to run for ten years, or until 1926, with the provision that it could be renewed for ten years more at the request of either party. Ten months afterwards it was renewed for this additional decade by a joint memorandum of the two departments of state, although this extension was never ratified by the legislative branch of either country. We also dissolved one Congress which was somewhat hostile to the puppet president, Dartiguenave, and Franklin D. Roosevelt, then assistant secretary of the navy, drafted a new Constitution for Haiti which broke the precedent of over a hundred years and gave to foreigners the right to own land. When the Haitian Congress refused to ratify this Constitution, we dissolved the Congress; and since then there has been no Haitian Congress. We then submitted the Constitution to the voters for their approval, despite the fact that we now claim the Haitians are too illiterate to elect a Congress. Marines controlled the voting booths, and the voters were given a white ballot to cast which signified approval of the Constitution. It was claimed, however, that this was a perfectly fair election, since the voters were free to go to the armed marines and ask for the negative ballots. By such tactics, which the politicians of Chicago might well envy, we declared the Constitution had been ratified by a vote of 98,299 to 769.

If there is no Haitian Congress, what then is the Haitian government? There is a council of state of twenty-one members who are appointed by the President and hold office at his pleasure. They in turn elect the President. The ridiculous situation is thus presented of the President appointing the very men who elect him. Under these circumstances it was not surprising that Louis Borno, who was elected President in 1922, should have been re-elected in 1926.

In that year a number of Haitian women asked the Women's International League for Peace and Freedom to investigate the American occupation. Since the American branch of that organization had been active in trying to protect minorities, it was thought that they might well devote some attention to minorities which were closer at home. The American branch, with the co-operation of other organizations, sent such a commission to Haiti, which included among its members two Negroes. At the request of the American Friends Service Committee I served as a member of this commission to represent the Society of Friends, the Quakers.

In reality, of course, the Haitian government is but a shadow, and the real power is the United States. Behind the presidential palace are barracks, and in those barracks a regiment of marines is stationed. They prevent the President from being assassinated, and they enable the American High Commissioner, General Russell, to give the Haitians authoritative advice. No act can be passed of which he does not approve, and his will is virtually law. Americans control the chief departments of the government. This winter we succeeded in having an amendment to the Constitution passed which limited the tenure of the highest judges and which gave the President the power to replace them. In this way, we will secure control of the judiciary which hitherto has been pro-Haitian.

In fact, therefore, we have substituted a foreign military dictatorship for a series of domestic ones. We have given the Haitians relative freedom from revolutions by the heavy arm of our military power, we have collected funds honourably, we have built roads and, best of all, have established an admirable system of hospitals and clinics. But, on the other hand, we have done nothing to develop democratic institutions, and we have affronted the nationalistic and racial pride of the educated Haitians. We built many of the roads with forced labour in the early days of the occupation, and this led to a revolt on the part of the people which was put down with great bloodshed, and during which atrocities were undoubtedly committed by our troops, as is almost inevitable in such cases. We have compelled Haiti to pay dubious claims for a railway whose contract was secured by Americans through graft and which has benefitted American banking interests. We have not given the popular schools sufficient funds. Our officers there have all too frequently had strong racial prejudices which have embittered the relations between the Haitians and the occupation. Most of all, the fact that the occupation rests on force has made the Haitians distinctly restive under our control and in the main anxious to see it removed.

The United States must choose whether it wishes to go on with an imperialistic program or whether it wishes to allow the Haitians to govern themselves as quickly as possible.   If we desire the latter, then we should have a bona-fide Congress elected immediately, which would draft a home-made Constitution and elect its own President.   Then by training more Haitians in the government services and by withdrawing the marines, we could restore Haiti to the rank of an independent nation.   Personally, I have no doubt that this is the more correct policy to follow, since it will help to lessen the opposition of South and Central America to us and pave the way for a true Pan-Americanism which would be based upon the co-operation of all the republics of this hemisphere and not upon our own will alone.

May I, in conclusion, suggest that those who wish to inform themselves about Haiti may do so by reading Blair Niles' very interesting book, *Black Haiti*, together with H. P. Davis' excellent *Black Democracy*. The report of our commission, *Occupied Haiti*, edited by Miss Emily Balch, has been published by the Writers Publishing Company.

XXIV

A WELCOME TO NANKING

EDITH M. PYE *is an English Quaker nurse who was head of the Quaker Maternity Hospital in the Marne during the war. Under her this hospital almost at the battle line achieved an efficiency, measured by low death rate, unequalled in the best city hospitals of the world. As a result of her work there she wears the red ribbon of the Legion of Honour. She has also been head of one of the great associations of nurses in England. In 1927 she was sent by the Women's International League for Peace and Freedom, together with Mme. Drevet, as a messenger to the women of China, bearing messages of sympathy, interest and good will from the women of the west.*

These messengers visited French Indo-China, as well as many other parts of China, going even as far as Hankow. Everywhere they found the warmest welcome from the people. Only governments suspected them and apparently feared them, governments accustomed to deal with people by force rather than through sympathetic human interest. Miss Pye's story told here is the story of Nanking as she saw it shortly after Europeans had been killed there.

YOU must not go to Nanking; it is not safe," they said to us on our arrival at Shanghai. "Nanking is where they have massacres." We were a delegation of women sent by the Women's International League for Peace and Freedom to bring to women in China messages of sympathy, interest and

good will from their western sisters, to learn from them
about the women's movement and to find out how we
could work together to promote international peace
and friendship.

We had the friendliest welcome in Shanghai, and
when the women of Nanking sent one of their number
down specially to invite us to visit the capital of the
Nationalist government, the southern government, we
did not hesitate to accept. The train that took us
there was a perfectly good train and arrived only a
little late. We were met by a group of about six members of a committee, in native Chinese clothes, representing all the women's organizations in the town
and province—a committee which had been specially
formed to make arrangements for us. They had borrowed two of the government motor-cars and had
stretched across the back of each a banner bearing the
words: " Welcome to the delegates of the Women's
International League for Peace and Freedom," in both
English and Chinese.

So warm was our welcome that we felt at once that
we had done right to come. These little Chinese ladies
had done everything they could think of to show us
how glad they were to have us among them and, before
the stay was over, we were sure we were among
friends; we felt affection and understanding had been
growing up between us. They had arranged for us to
stay at Ginling College for Women, which is the off-
spring of Smith College (American) and whose Chinese
staff, in spite of youth and inexperience, had been able
unassisted to carry on the work through those months

of anxiety during the summer. Now, however, some of the more experienced American staff had gone quietly back to share the burden which was too heavy for those young shoulders to bear alone for more than a short time.

We drove through the dry dust-coloured fields and past grey stone buildings. Armed soldiers were everywhere, in every nook and cranny, and we were carried back at once in memory to those little French towns behind the lines in France. Nanking was exactly like them, with the same problems and the same difficulties of a country at war.

At Ginling we had more welcome, from the faculty, both Chinese and American, and we spent the evening hearing of the way the beautiful buildings had been saved, how occupation by the military was prevented. We were told of the fine work being done there in the education of Chinese women who will be the leaders of the women's movement of the future. The next day our Chinese friends came to fetch us, having again borrowed motors bearing Nationalist flags with the white star on the blue ground. They took us to the Foreign Office, where about forty of the leading women met us.

A luncheon was arranged in our honour and, as is usual in China, the reception and visiting came first. It was a marvel to us how many of the Chinese women spoke English. The chairman of the women's department for the province was quite young and really anxious to learn all we could tell her of women's work in the west, as indeed they all appeared to be. It was not our first attempt at Chinese food. By that time we could even manage to eat with chop-sticks the delicious dish of shrimps and peas, which was one of the seemingly endless procession of good things to eat. After the sweet, the dessert, we ended up with the " chrysanthemum " dish, a shallow chafing-dish filled with soup which is boiled on the table and into which all the choicest morsels of game, meat and tender vegetables are thrown raw, and cooked before the guests, the flames leaping out through the perforated alcohol lamp and surrounding the dish like the petals of a golden flower.

From the luncheon we all went in procession to the hall of Nanking University, where a public meeting had been arranged. We were a little taken aback at the honour of being " played in " by a military band whose members then quietly sat down to listen to what we had to say about peace. And it must be confessed that we spoke more about the positive side of the building up of international friendships and understanding than of the abolition of the military profession. The meeting began with the reading of Sun Yat Sen's will, and then all turned and saluted his portrait on the wall, bowing three times. Our chairman was a very able young woman doing important work in the department of education. She made an excellent peace speech in introducing us, which was evidently listened to with attention.

After the speaking was over, a Chinese lady sang a western song in an exquisite voice, and a flute player played for us on two different flutes. The first, he

said, made a very small sweet sound, and its name in
Chinese was Peace. The second had large holes
through which the wind came freely, and the name of
that one was Freedom; and that was why he had
chosen them as instruments to play to the delegates
of the Women's International League for Peace and
Freedom!

The next day we were shown something of the valuable extension work that is carried on by the universi-
ties in the hope of abating some of the terrible poverty
of the countryside. Farmers are taught how to produce better crops and better cotton. Educational
posters, very beautifully painted by hand, are used
very largely. Experimental work in agriculture is carried on at the same time, and there is real enthusiasm
among the Chinese staff entrusted with it.

In the afternoon we were received officially by the
municipality of Nanking, and found that we were again
expected to address a public meeting of citizens, very
much more numerous than before. After we had
spoken, the mayor of Nanking addressed the meeting;
also, the commissioner for education spoke, and votes
of thanks to us were very ably moved and seconded by
two women. Then we were led away—not to have our
heads chopped off, as our timourous European friends
in Shanghai might have feared, but to be photographed
together with the Chinese women and to be given a
wonderful tea with coffee as a special delicacy.

We visited the Y. W. C. A. hotel, now of course
entirely Chinese, and we were much interested to learn
that many of the women working in the Nationalist

government offices lived there in the closest and friendliest relation with the Y. W. C. A. secretaries. The
social work undertaken by the members of the Y. W.
C. A. had begun again. The little bath-house for
women, with its neat cubicles and wooden bath-tubs,
gives the comfort of a hot bath to as many as forty
women in an afternoon. The little school, robbed of
its furniture during the disturbances of the spring, had
been re-opened, the children having to content themselves with tiny stools in place of their desks. " We
believe that Christianity means service to others," the
workers said, and they are literally carrying out their
faith in a spirit of peace and good will to all.

We were taken to see a country school, far away
from any western influence, where the children danced
and sang for us charmingly. We sat among the other
children as audience, and their eager pleasure and
sharp comments (translated for us by our friends)
gave a sense of intelligence and friendliness that is
delightful to look back upon.

We saw a rural school for teachers where young men
and women were learning together the elements of
farming, so that they could teach it to their future
pupils. These young people, both university and middle school graduates, did all their own housework, besides the digging of the ground for cultivation. The
girls had a little house to live in, but the boys had
overflowed theirs, and some slept in tents, winter
weather notwithstanding. Their gay and cheerful
comradeship and enthusiasm was indeed a sign of the
times—the new spirit in China.

The Purple Mountain, looked up to and loved by all who live in Nanking, contains the tombs of the Ming emperors and is to be the last resting-place of Sun Yat Sen's body. We were taken out to see the extraordinary engineering feat that is required to construct the shrine on the side of the mountain. Granite and marble is carried there by human labour, only the very largest blocks being conveyed up the steep paths by bullock cart. Myriads of men are quietly and industriously carrying baskets of débris down the great stairway half completed. The forestry department has plans for gardens and great avenues of trees to make a fitting tomb for the man who spent his energy and life in unselfish devotion to the cause of the people, and who is loved, venerated and even worshipped by them.

Our visit came to an end, and we left Nanking feeling that understanding and sympathy had grown deeper during our daily contacts. It is our hope that some day these may be renewed.

XXV

ADVENTURES THAT HAVE NOT BEEN TOLD

EDWARD THOMAS, *the editor of the series, in this final chapter summarizes a number of stories of Quaker adventures which he deems needed to complete the picture of the series and for which he was unable to secure speakers who could tell the stories out of their personal recollections.*

IN planning these talks I had hoped to have as a speaker some one who had seen the Quaker wedding in Poland, but as that was not possible I will repeat the story as I have heard it told.

The story begins when the cry from Russia, " Hunger is coming! " reached Durnstein, the village on the banks of the Danube, where the Duke of Austria kept Richard the Lion-Hearted prisoner for three years. In that village two Quaker workers, a college student and a young girl (a registered nurse) were spending well-earned vacations. For a year and a half they had worked together, and come to know each other through experiences with human suffering in fighting famine, typhus and tuberculosis among the war refugees in Poland. They knew what " hunger in Russia " meant. Their hearts were stirred by the call. Russia was said to be a country of danger and uncertainty, and they felt they could face the risks of work in Russia with more courage if they were married.

The next day after the call came they started on the long journey to Warsaw. There, in the office of the American consul, they learned that Poland was not a Gretna Green, for the consul said: " I cannot marry you. It would be a civil marriage, and such are illegal in Poland. Why don't you have a church wedding? "

" Would a Quaker wedding, in Poland, be legal? "

" No," said the consul, " only marriages by the larger established churches are valid here, such as the Roman or Greek Catholic, and a few others."

" Where can we get a civil marriage that will be recognized as legal? "

" You might go to Germany, or France, but you would have to live there several months. Why don't you go to Danzig? Danzig is newly established as a free city under the rule of the League of Nations. Its marriage laws are probably quite flexible. It is only a night's ride from here."

They went to Danzig, the ancient free city, the great Baltic port of the Middle Ages. The American consul there told them that the stadtsbeamter was the one man who could help them, and that that gentleman could be found in the old City Hall, with its single tower visible from all parts of the city.

Leaving the consul's office, they walked through twisting streets, past halls of the merchant guilds of the Middle Ages, across bridges over canals, past the sixteenth century crane tower, the model for the steam cranes of today, beside churches with clanging chimes, until the massive tower of the City Hall rose above them.

The stadtsbeamter was a fatherly, grey-haired, old man who quickly lost his military reserve when he saw the red and black Quaker stars on the left sleeves of the young people's coats. The student had to act as interpreter, as the nurse did not speak German. " Yes," said the old man, " I would marry you at once, but the fundamental law of Danzig states that you must reside here two weeks before you can be married. Danzig is a homelike city to stay in. You will find it a pleasure to be here for two weeks, and today for a beginning you shall dine with me at my home. My relatives in Germany write me about the Quaker feeding there. Every one in Germany knows about it. So the Quakers are going to do for Russia what they have done for Germany. People are starving to death in Russia—aren't you afraid to go? No? You were the first to come to Germany after the war when no one else would come; you are afraid of nothing. Where will you stop? "

The student interrupted the old man, saying that they must go to Russia at once; two weeks' delay was too long—more would starve. " Can you not make an exception, Herr Beamter, in this case, and let us be married at once? " he asked.

The stadtsbeamter resumed his dignity. " Is it for me to set aside the fundamental law of the city? I cannot do it." Then he remembered he was speaking to Quaker workers. He resumed: " There is the stadtsinspektor. I will speak to him. If he is willing, he and I will appear in person before the Senate, which meets tomorrow morning, and ask them for a special act to meet this urgent case.   Come back at eleven tomorrow."

The young people wondered what the action of the Senate would be, or if the League of Nations, from which the Senate of Danzig derives its authority, would have to be consulted.   What actually happened they never knew.   They only knew that when they appeared before the stadtsbeamter the next morning, the old man smiled upon them and told them he was ready to marry them.   He led them to a large audience chamber and, seating them on a bench, he mounted a dais before them and impressively began the civil ritual.

The nurse knew only two words of German, *Ja* and *Nein*.   She sat in rapt attention, holding them in readiness to use at the proper moment when the stadtsbeamter should have finished his long preliminary speech.   She did not know that he had come to the end of it, and so, when he looked at her directly and said something in a very impressive and awe-inspiring tone she felt he must be warning her not to fall into some of the pitfalls that surround the path of matrimony.   She replied with a modest, but firm, "*Nein.*"   All laughed, including herself, when the student turned to her rescue, saying that the stadtsbeamter had simply asked her if she promised to be a faithful, loving and obedient wife.   She quickly changed her reply, and the ceremony soon came to an end.   The old man gave them his warmest blessing, and they left the City Hall.

They did not yet consider themselves married, however, but looked forward to the time when their real marriage would take place five days later in the Quaker Meeting at Warsaw.

When they reached Warsaw urgent calls separated them. The nurse went to a fellow-worker, ill with typhus, and the student went to the Russian frontier to expedite a train-load of supplies for the starving Russians.

The night of the fourth day he returned. The next day the Quaker workers of that part of Poland were seated in a silent, reverent meeting with their Polish friends, some of whom had come a night's journey from Krakow. Before this group the student and nurse stood up, and he, taking her hand, said: " In the presence of God and before these witnesses, I take thee to be my wife, promising to be unto thee a loving and faithful husband as long as we both shall live." And she, taking his hand, said: " In the presence of God and before these witnesses I take thee to be my husband, promising to be unto thee a loving and faithful wife as long as we both shall live."

The meeting was again silent, then was broken by a few words, from their friends, of blessing and encouragement for those who had chosen to walk together on the road of service and danger. After the meeting all present signed the marriage certificate. A few days later the student and nurse, as man and wife, started on their way to Moscow.

Some stories of Quaker adventure cannot be told by the actors in them until new governments arise. These are stories about political refugees.

In one country news came to the government officials
of many shots fired in the streets of a village in a
cavernous limestone country. No one was reported to
have been hit, but the government officials sent a squad
of soldiers to arrest those guilty of firing the shots and
to punish them. On arriving at the village, the soldiers
demanded that a certain brilliant young man surrender
himself to them as guilty. The young man and his
friends had expected this demand, for he was widely
known for his outspoken opposition to the governmental authorities; the youth had disappeared into
one of the numerous caverns. So the soldiers established a watch in the village around the house of the
young man's family and quartered themselves on the
village.

Near the village was living a Quaker well known for
his relief work in time of famine, and respected by all
the people and by the authorities. To him the young
man came by night for advice and help, and for news
of his family.

The Quaker saw that the presence of the soldiers
was galling to the villagers and likely to lead to trouble.
From the officer in command he ascertained that the
government would be satisfied if the young man would
go through the form of imprisonment for a single day.
When the Quaker next saw the young man he prevailed
upon him to yield himself to the soldiers in the presence of the Quaker for the single day's imprisonment.
The agreement was carried out by both sides, the government and the military gloried in the fancied re-
establishing of their prestige, and the young man

became the hero of the village for having suffered persecution to rid it of soldiers.

I wish, also, that I could show you a motion-picture
I really have seen; the motion-picture of the Polish
Christmas tree of 1922, the first Christmas tree the children of the village had gazed on for eight years. So
great was the joy over that tree, so overpowering the
tears in the eyes of the old folks, the open-mouthed
wonder and eager whisperings and excited shoutings of
the children, that the Quaker workers built a sled, and
on it erected the Christmas tree with its decorations. To
the sled they harnessed four white horses. Then they
drove it over the snow through the pine forests to one
village after another, as long as the tree and its decorations could be held together, until the tree had been
seen by the children of twenty-seven villages, telling
the children that Christmas had really come back to
the earth.

I wish I could bring to this country some of the
younger English Quakers and have them tell you how
they went out in the very beginning of the war as unarmed ambulance workers. How they found hundreds
of cases of typhoid fever in Ypres—and all news of
the epidemic suppressed by the military authorities.
How the municipal authorities had deserted the city,
leaving hundreds, perhaps thousands, living in the cellars and ruins of the shell-torn city. How these young
men established a hospital, where they cared for seven
hundred of the typhoid fever patients; how they vac-
cinated twenty-six thousand more against typhoid, thus
stamping out that dread disease. How they admin-

istered the city government themselves; and how, when the war was over, they went quietly home to humdrum lives.

Sometimes the Quaker work seemed to bring no promise of reward. One of the young men who opened the Berlin office for child feeding was sent down to Hamburg to receive the first food shipment. During the long railroad journey he wondered how he and his fellow-workers could use the great opportunity open to them, how they could face the many new problems. He expected to receive thousands of barrels of flour. In Hamburg, to his horror, they offered him a thousand barrels of whiskey, something that seemed little better than poison when it came to a country starved for lack of the grain from which whiskey was made. He had not thought of the problem of straightening out the mistakes of people whom he never saw, mistakes that might cost many lives.

The women relief workers, too, faced their disappointments. One group opened a large case in one of the clothing shipments sent by another agency and found it full of second-hand wigs, the discard of a beauty parlour, utterly useless on the steppes of Russia to which the case had been brought by great exertions.

But elsewhere, and in many places, the workers knew they had an exceedingly great reward,—thankfulness in the hearts of the people around them; many rewards, indeed, each in its way as great as the reward that came to the young man and young woman who were married in Danzig. In the city of Gotha a Quaker worker received one day a new kind of coin

in change. On looking carefully he found it was a
fifty-pfennig piece with the words *Quaker Dank,*
Quaker thanks, stamped on its terra cotta body. It
was about the size of an American nickel, and bore
the crossed-sword trademark of the royal Dresden
pottery.

Another worker received a new kind of fifty-pfennig
paper note bearing on its face a sketch of the city.
When he turned the note over he saw in the centre a
picture of a steaming bowl with a nurse dealing soup
out to emaciated children at the right, and a picture
of a man at the left with a loaf of bread and a knife in
his left hand, while with his right hand he was holding
out a slice of bread to a child. And above and below
the picture were the lines of a poem:

> " *Saint Augustine once in time of need*
> *Did the hungry Gotha children feed.*
> *Today with holy bread from distant lands*
> *The Quakers fill the hungry children's hands.*"

And beneath the poem the Quaker worker saw the
same red and black star that he wore on the left sleeve
of his coat.

Still another kind of money appeared in change—a
ninety-pfennig note bearing the same poem. Beneath
the arches of a railroad bridge which supports the
tablet bearing the poem, there appear other children
gathered around a nurse and doctor, while in the back-
ground is seen a steamship bearing food for the railroad to bring to the children.

Sometimes the opportunities for helping the sufferers after the war came in the most unexpected ways.

On some farms, especially in Ruthenia, the Quakers found at most but a single tool left, a hoe, or spade, and the peasant farmer and his wife had to take turns using the tool to be able to cultivate the ground to the best advantage. The Quakers discovered that it was possible to supply the country with the farming tools which it had seemed impossible to obtain. They found that the Reparations Commission after the war was selling German trench spades in places where there was no market for them, getting about two to four cents apiece for an excellent tool costing more than a dollar to make. These spades the workers diverted to the needy farmers, and earned their eternal gratitude.

In the city of Frankfurt-am-Main the bread cards for the four weeks, August 2 to 29, 1921, bore a picture of a figure like the conventional one of William Penn, one hand on the head of a child and the other dealing out soup with a ladle. Under the picture was the legend, " Thanks for the Quaker Help."

But the great reward, the one that came nearest to the heart of one worker, was not on the bread cards, nor on the money, nor in the newspapers, nor in the formal resolutions of governmental authorities. That reward came in the unstudied words of a little child.

On the morning of the day she was to leave the city after her term of service was over, her office secretary came in a little late, with a strange look on her face, saying, " You can't guess what happened this morning.   My little boy came in crying bitterly, terribly excited.   I tried in vain for a long time to quiet him. Finally he said, 'Oh, mother, I saw what was almost an awful accident!   A great big motor truck was coming down the street, and—and—it hit a little boy, and knocked him down, and it would have run over him, but a Quaker ran out and saved him.'

"I said to him, 'My dear, what makes you think it was a Quaker?'

"He looked up at me and said, 'It *must* have been a Quaker—because—Mother, isn't it the Quakers who take care of little children?'"

I am looking forward to the time when America will be ready to send forth volunteers to serve other people in times of distress or disaster, as ready as it has hitherto been to protect selfish economic interests,— the time when America will be willing to spend as much for helping other people as it is now ready to spend on a greater navy, or on tobacco, or on chewing-gum.

Then, some day, a little child, helped by America, will say, "Mother, it *must* have been an American! Because, mother, isn't it the Americans that take care of little children?"

Printed in the United States of America

Printed in the United States
118752LV00009B/79/A